*What has been is what will be,
and what has been done is what will be done;
and there is nothing new under the sun.*
❧ Ecclesiastes 1:9

*And the One who sat upon the throne said,
"Behold, I make all things new."*
❧ Revelation 21:5

*You have become a new creation
And have clothed yourself in Christ.*
❧ Celebration of Baptism

Dedicated to my mother
Irene M. Graham
in anticipation of her eighty-fourth birthday
with gratitude and love
for she "has filled the hungry
with good things" (Luke 1:53).

Excerpts from the English translation of *Rite of Baptism for Children* ©1969, International Committee on English in the Liturgy, Inc. (ICEL); excerpts from the English translation the *The Roman Missal* ©1973, ICEL; exerpts from the English translation of *Order of Christian Funerals* ©1985, ICEL. All rights reserved.

Twenty-Third Publications
A Division of Bayard
One Montauk Avenue, Suite 200
New London, CT 06320
(860) 437-3012 or (800) 321-0411
www.23rdpublications.com

Copyright ©2007 William C. Graham. No part of this publication may be reproduced in any manner without prior written permission of the publisher. Write to the Permissions Editor.

Most of the Scripture passages contained herein are from the *New Revised Standard Version of the Bible*, copyright ©1989, by the Division of Christian Education of the National Council of Churches in the U.S.A. All rights reserved.

ISBN 978-1-58595-632-6
Library of Congress Catalog Card Number: 2007930685
Printed in the U.S.A.

CONTENTS

ACKNOWLEDGMENTS	v
INTRODUCTION: CHANGES AND CHALLENGES	1
PART ONE: BAPTISMAL DIGNITY	
Who Do You Think You Are?	14
Who Is the Greatest?	19
An Unrestricted Spirit	24
Claiming a Path	29
PART TWO: LIVING THE LIFE OF JESUS	
Jesus and the Reign of God	36
Imagination and Hope	45
Sensitivity to the Poor	48
Gestures of Compassion	51
PART THREE: THE LIFE OF PRAYER	
What We Dare to Say!	56
Intercessory Prayer	62
The Eucharist and Our Ministry	66
PART FOUR: FEASTS AND SEASONS	
Smoke and Ashes	72
Lent: Power and Joy	76
A Time for Resurrection	80
The Paschal Mystery	83

Part Five: Seeking a Spirituality

    Unity and Charity   94

    Standing for Human Dignity   99

    "Manner" and Manners   103

Part Six: Steadfastness

    Marriage and Spirituality   110

    Keeping the Faith   116

    Serving One Another   122

Part Seven: Ritual as Teacher

    The Burial of a Pope   126

    Burdens Lifted   129

Part Eight: Seeking Clarity

    Contemporary Issues   138

    The Eucharist and the Church   146

    Challenges on the Horizon   153

Conclusion: Watch, Serve, Study, and Pray   160

ACKNOWLEDGMENTS

I want to express my gratitude to all of those who have formed me in faith, in service, in prayer, and in academic study; my colleagues both in ministry and in the academy whose thoughts and observations and questions have prompted me to think, observe, and study more wisely; Chicagoland's Lewis University where while serving as professor of theology and chair of the theology department, I began this manuscript, and to its Dean's Fund which funded part of my work, and to Dr. Katherine Delaney, then the ever-supportive dean who initiated the fund; Fr. Thomas Gross and Mrs. Barbara Akeo (may she be with God) and my friends at St. John Vianney Parish in Kailua, Oʻahu, Hawaiʻi, for providing a place of light, happiness, and peace in which I did the final editing of this work; Mary Carol Kendzia and Gwen Costello at Twenty-Third Publications, for their interest, enthusiasm, and guidance in this project. I am especially grateful to the students in ministry, particularly those at Caldwell College in New Jersey where I was privileged to begin a new degree program in pastoral ministry, the first graduates of which have revealed themselves to be outstanding women and men of faith and service. While the insights of these people have shaped this work, any deficiencies here are my responsibility alone.

Many of the following chapters were originally published in various forms or pieces in a variety of publications. I am grateful to those editors for permission to republish edited versions of my earlier work.

Part of the Introduction was originally published in a review of *Lay Leaders of Worship: A Practical and Spiritual Guide*, by Kathleen Hope Brown, in *Ministry and Liturgy*.

A variant of "Claiming a Path" was first published as "Spike and the Diminished Body of Christ" in *America* (November 23, 1996).

A variant of "Who Do You Think You Are?" was first published in *Ministry and Liturgy* (December 1999/January 2000).

A variant of "Sensitivity to the Poor" was originally published as "Pondering the Sublime Dignity of All Humans," in *National Catholic Reporter* (November 3, 2000).

A variant of "What We Dare to Say!" was first published *Celebration* (February 1999) and later as a chapter in *Sacred Adventure: Beginning Theological Study*, by William C. Graham (University Press of America, 1999).

"Jesus and the Reign of God" was first published as a chapter in *Sacred Adventure: Beginning Theological Study*. "The Social Aims of Jesus," a chapter in Walter Rauschenbusch's *Christianity and the Social Crisis* (Louisville: Westminster/John Knox, 1991; originally published in 1907) provided an outline and inspiration for this essay.

A shorter version of "Intercessory Prayer" was first published as "Needful Prayer" in *The Priest* (March 2000).

"Imagination and Hope" was first published in *Today's Parish*.

A variant of "Gestures of Compassion" was published as "Choosing: to be Effective, Anti-abortion Teaching Must Both Inform and Affirm" in *Celebration* (March 2003).

"The Eucharist and Ministry" was originally published as a chapter in *Sacred Adventure: Beginning Theological Study*.

A variant of "Up in Smoke and Ashes" was first published in *Modern Liturgy* (December 1997/January 1998).

"Lent: Power and Joy" was published as "The Power of Peace: National Policy based on Firepower Avoids Deeper Challenges" in *Celebration* (July 1999).

"A Time for Resurrection" was first published in *Today's Parish*.

"The Paschal Mystery" was first published in *Ministry and Liturgy* (February 2006); the conclusion was published as "Ritual as Teacher" in *Celebration* (January 2006).

A variant of "Standing for Human Dignity" was published as "The Preacher and the Abortion Opponent" in *Celebration* (September 1998).

The Road to Holiness Through Wholeness was originally published as "Silent Vigil" in *Celebration* (December 2000).

"Ad Astra per Aspera: A Summer's Journey to Restored Faith" was published in *Ministry and Liturgy* (August 2004).

A variant of "Serving One Another" was published as "Clerk's enthusiasm for boy's adventure extends Christ's hand" in *National Catholic Reporter* (September 27, 2002).

A variant of "The Burial of a Pope" was published as "Theologians, sociologists and historians will interpret John Paul II's popularity," *Duluth News Tribune*, April 20, 2005.

A variant of "Burdens Lifted" was published as "Sure and Certain Hope," in *Celebration, A Comprehensive Worship Resource*, published by *National Catholic Reporter* (November 2005).

A version of "Seeking Clarity" was published as "A Little Help Here! A Teacher's Plea to the Bishops" in *Listening* (Spring 2002).

A version of "Challenges on the Horizon" was published as a two-part series "Explosions and explosives: Lay pastoral ministry in the new century" (*Ministry and Liturgy*, March 2003), and "Explosions and explosives: Lay pastoral ministry in the new century" (*Ministry and Liturgy*, April 2003).

Parts of "Watch, Serve, Study, and Pray" were published as "Crafting a Spirituality for Ministry" in *Ministry and Liturgy* (December 2006) and "Polished Arrows" in *Celebration: an ecumenical worship resource* from *National Catholic Reporter* (November 2006).

⁂ WILLIAM C. GRAHAM

INTRODUCTION

Changes and Challenges

*And let us not grow weary in well-doing,
for in due season we shall reap,
    if we do not lose heart.
So then, as we have opportunity,
    let us do good to all,
and especially to those who are of the household of faith.*
— Galatians 6:9–10

A perceived change is evident in the Roman Catholic community as well as in many other Christian communions as we reevaluate and return to our roots. Women and men, neither ordained nor members of the traditional religious communities of priests, brothers, or sisters, both in numbers and in ways not seen or experienced before in living memory, are undertaking ministry. Some people find this confusing or frightening and pray all the harder for vocations, without realizing that their prayers are perhaps being answered, but in a way that is not in keeping with the specifics of their petitions. God is indeed raising up ministry and ministers in the church, and while there are fewer ordained and vowed people in service to the growing and developing church, there is no shortage at all either of ministers or ministry. This might seem new, something of a major change. It is more a return to the way things once were in the very beginning (consider the division of labor in the Acts of the Apostles, for example).

Today's new pastoral ministers are undertaking their tasks not in place of priests but side by side with priests, involved in many aspects and areas in which they have both special competence and a specific vocation. ==You who undertake these ministries do so as a consequence of your baptismal commitment.== Your dignity comes from Christ who claims us and commissions us to "go out and teach all nations" (Matthew 28:19).

So who am I to write for you? As a diocesan priest, I enjoyed ten years and seventeen days as a pastor and look on that era as a special time of grace. Since then, I have been in college and university classrooms, teaching in four different graduate programs of pastoral ministry, and two programs that do not grant degrees, from Long Island to Hawaii. I feel that I know you, the students and the ministers, as well as the folks in the pews, the problems and the possibilities. I hope that my own experiences, study, and pastoral and theological reflections will assist you, my colleagues in ministry with whom I am privileged to serve.

A word, then, about voice: I am clearly a pastoral minister, though not a lay minister. Sometimes I make reference to "we" or "us" and sometimes to "you." I trust that the distinction is evident and helpful. Please forgive what may occasionally seem awkward construction as I speak of "all of us ministers" or "we ministers" when I mean all ministers, and "you" or "lay ecclesial ministers" or "lay pastoral ministers" when I mean you, the target audience.

"What do we call you, anyway?" is a question pastoral ministers sometimes hear. They are usually Mrs. or Ms.; sometimes Mr.; and, occasionally Dr. But these ministers do not come equipped with a pastoral title as do the Fathers, the Sisters, and the Brothers. But what to call you is only one of the concerns (and most folks figure that out in a heartbeat anyway). We will here use the terms lay ministers, lay ecclesial ministers, and lay pastoral ministers interchangeably.

A New Generation

Hearing and recognizing your call as part of this new generation of ministers, you no doubt seek guidance as you grow into your role.

Programs of preparation have been springing up rapidly in dioceses across the United States, and Catholic colleges, universities, and seminaries are pioneering new programs for academic study and training in practical skills. This is a new phenomenon in a healthy, developing church. It is in keeping with the best interpretations of gospel mandates and conciliar and post-conciliar documents. Because this movement within ministry is new and still developing, we can understand that those involved in the programs of preparation might feel as did those involved in the formation of seminaries after the Council of Trent. It was a good idea then, as the Council fathers reacted to the obvious needs of the church for a better educated clergy. Today, in the best educated church ever to exist anywhere on earth, a new but similar development is underway. Thousands of pastoral ministers are busy about their tasks with eagerness and joy. But sometimes confidence does not match enthusiasm. Perhaps the new director of the RCIA was last year a third-grade teacher, and the youth minister has a bachelor's degree in business or perhaps Spanish literature. They may study in a diocesan or university program, understanding that their ministry is good work, but that with a firmer theological foundation they would both be and feel better equipped to meet the demands of the day.

Pastoral ministers, when employed full time, will certainly cost the church more than did the generations of Sisters and Brothers who built the vast network of Catholic schools, an enormous school system in the United States, second in size only to the public school systems. Those vowed folks, joined by the occasional lay teacher, were largely volunteer labor. The new generation of pastoral workers, with families, mortgages, and other obligations, cannot be volunteers. Scripture speaks authoritatively to their situation: "The laborer deserves to be paid" (1 Timothy 5:18). These ministers deserve, too, to be educated in a manner and place appropriate to their call and station. Programs and resources for academic and spiritual formation and ongoing development are clearly in order. Those who find a vocation in lay ministry must speak out about needs and challenges, remembering that this ministry is a response to the call of Baptism.

Asking for resources and respect is not out of order. Blessed John XXIII, of happy memory, wrote in his encyclical *Pacem in Terris*: "Those who discover that they have rights have the responsibility to claim them."

But what about spiritual development? Many who run the programs of academic formation for lay ministers recognize that they are not seminaries and that the students they accept tend to be adults who, presumably, have already been formed in the practice of their faith. Whence will come ongoing spiritual direction and impetus, not to mention resources, for spiritual growth? These are issues yet to be addressed definitively. In periods of rapid growth and change, all matters cannot be settled at once. *The Church in the Modern World* (*Gaudium et spes*) speaks to the issue of ongoing development in decreeing that "new conditions in the end affect the religious life itself." Development of and in lay ministry is clearly the work of God's good Spirit, and we, all of us, are called to cooperation.

This book is written in grateful recognition of the growth that is underway among lay people and in our ecclesial institutions. The reign of God is present, and lay ministers are the seeds of its future growth. Those already in ministry, some well formed and educated, and others still on the way, seek and deserve celebration of their activities and worth, with challenges and support from the rest of us to ensure that development is ongoing. I write here of the dignity of the call to lay ministry, the opportunities and problems of lay ministers that need attention, the challenges to lay ministers that can enrich days and decades with a careful attention to the presence of God's grace. This book is for you, that new breed, the new generation of lay church workers in the Catholic communion and in other Christian churches as well. My hope is that you will find your own concerns mirrored here, with suggestions for growth, questions for consideration, plans for prayer, prompts for study, and paths to peace.

We ministers—lay and ordained alike—move on then in lives of prayer and service. We recognize that the busyness of life causes us to move rapidly from concern to concern, sometimes with friction at our heels. Sometimes we wonder if our prayer life is as strong as our burdens demand it be. We remember the dictum of St. Benedict, who wrote "The Holy Rule for Monasteries," that we are to work and pray, so that the prayer of our lips perfects the work of our hands. We make peace with disturbances in our prayer life by recalling St. Vincent de Paul's comforting caution: "Do not become upset or feel guilty because you interrupted your prayer to serve the poor. God is not neglected if you leave him for such service. One of God's works is merely interrupted so that another can be carried out."

We read in the book of Revelation, "Another angel with a golden censer came and stood at the altar; he was given a great quantity of incense to offer with the prayers of all the saints on the golden altar that is before the throne. And the smoke of the incense, with the prayers of the saints, rose before God from the hand of the angel." Our efforts and our prayers, we believe, rise in the presence of God as sweet smelling incense. But Revelation continues: "Then the angel took the censer and filled it with fire from the altar and threw it on the earth; and there were peals of thunder, rumblings, flashes of lightning, and an earthquake" (8:3–5). There may be clashes and even thunderous roars, but if we are about God's work, seeking the truth, following the way, advancing God's reign, we will move in hope and confidence.

Possible Clashes

Let's consider some possible clashes or thunderous roars. Among them might be the way that we refer to God. I hope that references to God will not be a problem here. I consider inclusive language a very significant issue, but a linguistic and cultural issue, not a theological problem. More than half of pastoral ministers are women and many feel justifiably unhappy, confused, or disenfranchised by references to God as male. Language is evolving and we pastoral writers must shape a response that is helpful and challenging. We should not become part of the problem. If we render God neuter, avoiding any personal pronouns, we run the risk of making a linguistic problem into a theological issue by narrowing rather than broadening the avenues by which we come to God. We must not reinforce the mistaken idea that God is a male, but point instead to inclusiveness as a cohesive virtue for the body of Christ.

I hope we can also acknowledge difficulties where we find them in pastoral practice as well as in ecclesial issues, and not avoid admitting that we have difficulties in the church in our own era. There are very certain problems those involved in lay ministry are apt to encounter. For example, Kathleen Hope Brown, in *Lay Leaders of Worship: A Practical and Spiritual Guide* (Liturgical Press, 2004), writes for lay presiders of community prayer. In examining the kinds of relationships such leaders have to the communities from which they are called, she asks pertinent questions about skills, training, and credentials. She examines issues surrounding spiritual formation, and recognizing that lay ministry is here to stay, wisely asserts that her questions call for ongoing and careful consideration. There is much in the book that is both helpful and provocative. Her considerations about spirituality, formation, and continuing development of spirituality are, I think, very helpful not just for lay presiders but for all those who lead in liturgical and other ministerial capacities.

Brown begins and concludes with the lament that "lay leaders of prayer sometimes find their ministry questioned, objected to, and even openly opposed." She herself, just before her first service, was told, "That's all very nice, honey. Now, where's the priest?" The woman who asked the question perhaps pinpointed the idea to which Brown and other lay presiders need urgently to attend: There are instances in which they appropriately act as prayer leaders and in which they claim their rightful place among the people of God. There are other moments when they take the place of an absent priest. While she is correct that "lay presiders are not a stopgap solution to temporary need but a gift to the church for the long term," she and we must recognize the primacy of the Eucharist for the Sunday assembly. Lamenting its absence is not to disparage the one who fills in for the absent priest, but is an appropriate response. Better, it seems to me, is to concentrate on the many instances when it is entirely appropriate for a lay person to preside.

Two examples: The college where I currently teach is on the grounds of a Benedictine Monastery. I prayed vespers one recent evening with the Sisters in anticipation of a feast and the Prioress presided. It seemed entirely usual (because it is, in fact, entirely usual), and the blessing she imparted as we concluded bristled with the onrush of God's good Spirit. At a recent Mundelein gathering of the Pastoral Associates of the Archdiocese of Chicago at which I made a presentation, morning prayer was presided over by one of the participants who gave as fine a reflection on the morning's Scripture as I had heard in many months. No one could have asked where the priest was at either service; both women did as their office and community called them to do.

Brown points out that "lay preaching, until very recently, has been extremely rare and even now is not commonplace." But she cites another lay presider at the Children's Liturgy of the Word who later saw her five-year-old daughter delivering animated oratory into the bedroom mirror, explaining, "Mommy, I'm preaching—just like you!" This preacher wisely suggests that "perhaps the other little girls who participate in the Children's Liturgy of the Word will know from an early age that women can preach, can share the good news, and do it well."

This particular study would have been more helpful (and here is an agenda for some other lay minister's next book!) if it had delineated when lay presiders are appropriately put to work in graced moments in which they "give voice to the prayer of the community ... [leading] the community pastorally and reverently in an experience of worship" and when their presence will legitimately provoke the lament, "Wouldn't it be nice to have a priest?" Sunday without the Eucharist is a problem not the making of the lay presider, but she or he does preside in the lamentable absence of the priest.

Brown also relates the story of a lay presider who prepared and presided at a funeral service for an infant. Interestingly, though, she reports that "the pastor was supportive as he prayed with us as a community member." It seems very unusual for a pastor to attend a funeral at which a lay person presides, but she offers no explanation. Brown also fails to address when lay presiders ought to expect to be welcomed, and when they can legitimately be viewed as something other than what the church might expect. Not all lay ministers are liturgical ministers, but highlighting what remains unaddressed in her fine book suggests that there is much yet to be done in defining and recognizing ministries, in isolating problems, seeking solutions, and learning to live together in a way that seeks and serves the peaceable reign of God. As the church continues to reform, we will look for more of these kinds of reflections and guides, among which I hope my own book here is numbered, and can today be grateful for Brown's inspired insights and apt second name: Hope.

Reasons for Opposition

But sometimes lay leaders will find their ministry outside of preaching or presiding still questioned, objected to, and even openly opposed. It is important to understand some of the reasons that may be at play. One very bright and capable minister who holds a master of arts degree in pastoral ministry tearfully told me of her pastor who had demanded to see the papers she had written (and I had graded) in a summer seminar. She had earned a grade of A by virtue of careful reading, thoughtful analysis, finely tuned writing, and an insightfully prepared and well-presented project. He scanned what she presented and pronounced that had he been the professor, she would not have had the A. She was too hurt and flummoxed to recall that he had not in fact been the professor. He had not been the professor because her university did not hire people who hold the bachelor of science degree to teach graduate seminars in pastoral theology. He had not been successful in his own attempt to earn a master of arts and clearly (at least it seemed clear to me) felt some shame about this fact (and it was a fact, not a failure, as he seemed to fear). Apparently he felt the need to belittle his parishioner and coworker's efforts. He is not a bad man; he is a priest of considerable talent. My guess is that he felt uncomfortable having an employee and coworker who was not just a better student than he, but who held a more advanced academic degree.

The very first graduate student with whom I worked had her final project published by Liturgical Press. There was much rejoicing in her scholarly cohort and family. But her supervisor, a chancery official, took the news very hard and could not manage any congratulations at all. Her book came to the attention of another chancery half a continent away (priests are not always the villains; they are more often good readers, true talent scouts, and heroic coworkers). She was called for an interview and offered a better position in a more hospitable climate (both metaphorically and literally) even though she had not even been an applicant. She and her colleagues in lay ministry have recognized that a new and better education often leads to new employment and other opportunities. It is not so much that they outgrow their surroundings and colleagues, but that higher education is often threatening to undereducated supervisors and colleagues. One can understand why pastors or supervisors often hire workers whose credentials are limited: They are not just less expensive but also less threatening.

The academic dean of a seminary where lay people also study told me that the seminarians are often frustrated when studying side by side with lay students. When they wish to pull apart, they suggest that it is because of a need to build a priestly identity. There seem to be two issues at work here—or an issue and an excuse.

Issue one: Learning what it means to have a priestly identity is important for those who seek ordination. These candidates must observe, however, that even in a scandal-plagued church, we priests have a strong identity. We have a well-defined role in the ecclesial and civic communities. The ordination ceremony speaks volumes about who we are and how both church and self should understand that identity. The bishops give faculties and assignments. There is a special place where most priests live, dress that sets us apart in the sanctuary and on the streets, and formal terms of address. Ours is not a weak identity.

Issue two (the excuse): Studying scriptural pericopes or canon law with lay students will not impede the development of priestly identity. But to sit side by side with better students or harder workers, with folks who view themselves in a collegial and not subservient role, challenges us to ask what it means to serve as a priest in a church that is no longer one of immigrants and illiterates. The priest is no longer the only or best-educated person in a parish. We all, including and especially seminarians and others who aspire to ministry either lay or ordained, must understand, celebrate, and work with that understanding. Developing a priestly identity is a true concern both for seminarians and for those who form them; it is a concern for all the church as well, since we both seek and deserve competent, confident people serving in holy orders. The task is not just to craft and develop that identity, but also to distinguish between formation and fear. This, too, is part of our search for a spirituality that fits and forms.

Recognizing New Ministries

We who live in this extraordinarily well-educated church are coming more and more to recognize the ministries of those who serve us outside of holy orders. We do not have commissioning ceremonies for them, we are not sure exactly of what their titles should be, and we are not quite sure of how to pay a living wage (or even how to compute it fairly; since lay ministers live at home and not in rectories, their salaries cannot be compared to the priest's which includes a rectory, meals, and an amplitude of other considerations). We are not certain how to ensure just treatment in making contracts and terminating employment when necessary, or even what to do with their families when they are diversified through remarriage. All of these matters suggest a subject that needs to be midwifed into the imagination of the church: the future. Among the many tasks of the heroic lay ecclesial ministers is helping us keep one eye on our past and another on the future, that we might live daringly in the tension between what has gone before and what lies ahead. Think of Michelangelo's ceiling in the Sistine Chapel where God's finger reaches out toward Adam's. We must see ourselves as living in that space, in that tension. Learning to live there is to chart a spirituality for lay ministry.

Obviously enough, this book cannot address all of these difficulties. But it can point to the hope of justice that animates the church in every age. We are always a people passionately committed to justice (even when it takes us centuries to discover what justice might look like in a given instance), open to Benedict XVI's reminder that we are called to go beyond the minimal requirements of justice to the fullness of charity. This book, I hope, can also suggest a method for dealing with those opportunities and difficulties, a spirituality that will guide our feet in peaceful paths and our hearts to a more certain rhythm.

One of the techniques I employ here is a liberal use of quotes from both Scripture and church documents. I think the defining task of pastoral ministers is to dip into the church's treasury and make those treasures accessible to people who might otherwise not know them. So, rather than sending people to the Catechism or the ancient Christian writers, or even the Sacramentary, the pastoral minister uncovers and explicates the treasures found there. This is a hard sell in an era in which our culture tends to celebrate individual opinion as if it were on the plain of revelation, but this task is surely high among the duties of the church's ministers. It is a serviceable way, I think, to consider questions and concerns, and it suggests a manner in which together we can craft our own developing opinions in light of the sources available to us.

I hope that my experience can inform yours, so that you can, as Mary did, keep what is "treasure" and ponder these things in your hearts (Luke 2:19). I pray that these reflections find a home, promote thoughtful prayer and prayerful action, and that together we will labor and laugh until we, having seen removed all obstacles which might hinder us from receiving Christ with joy, merrily meet in heaven.

Next we will consider our identity as Christians and as ministers.

PART ONE

Baptismal Dignity

Who Do You Think You Are?

For he has looked with favor on the lowliness of his servant. ❧ LUKE 1:48

Those who work in programs of ministerial preparation are usually quick to suggest that pastoral ministers are a particularly blessed lot who keep visions of hopefulness alive. One professor reports leaning over to one of them during a convocation to inquire, "Where do you people get your hopefulness?" He was asked in return, "Who will separate us from the love of Christ?" (Romans 8:35).

One such pastoral minister, Joan, is bright and effervescent and multitalented. She is a director of religious education at a large Eastern parish where she also directs the RCIA and works with children in the Liturgy of the Word. She does many things and all of them well, and she also manages a family and a home. Her vision of where the church has been, where the church is today, and where the church may very well be called to be in the future is in keeping with the best interpretations of gospel mandates and conciliar and post-conciliar documents. Her biggest challenge in carrying out her vital ministry is her mother-in-law.

This mother-in-law is a Catholic woman of a particular age whose vision of the church was profoundly influenced by Barry Fitzgerald and Bing Crosby in the movie *Going My Way*. According to this woman, if something religious needs doing, a priest should do it. If Father is not doing it, perhaps he should get busy. If Father cannot or will not do it, let it be understood that the Holy Spirit has revealed that it didn't need to be done anyway. Joan and those other lay people who hear the call to ministry within their parish, in keeping with their baptismal dignity and the duties and responsibilities flowing therefrom, are dressed down with a single sarcastic question: "Who do you think you are?" As posed by the mother-in-law, the question is meant to bring any and all discussion to a halt.

Even if the question is asked in a mean-spirited and critical manner, however, it both begs and deserves an answer. Who does Joan think she is? And who do all lay ministers who seek to live out their baptismal commitment in service to the church think that they are? Joan is not the first to be asked such a question. Consider Mary coming to Elizabeth with the good news of the Incarnation. Elizabeth was tipped off to the wonder at her door by her son John who was at work as the forerunner of Jesus even before either of their births: "For behold," Elizabeth says to Mary, "when the voice of your greeting came to my ears, the babe in my womb leaped for joy" (Luke 1:44). Elizabeth said, "Blessed is she who believed that there would be a fulfillment of what was spoken to her from the Lord" (1:45). She did not ask, "Who do you think you are?" But don't you think someone else must have? If even Joseph seemed to have a hard time with the story of the angel's annunciation of an impending virgin birth and needed convincing by another angelic visit, there must have been any number of Nazarenes in the neighborhood who looked on the pregnant teenager as both manifestly sinful and distressingly prideful. Who could she think she was?

Who Was Jesus?

Perhaps it would be wise first to take the question and ask it of Jesus himself and those who first followed him. If we know who they thought they were, we pastoral ministers might be better equipped to answer the question about ourselves, and thus forge not just an identity but a deeper spirituality.

Remember Jesus and his beneficence in feeding the vast crowd when only five loaves and two fishes seemed to be available? He had just heard of the death of John the Baptist, and he withdrew in a boat to a deserted place by himself. But the eager crowds followed him on foot and greeted him as he disembarked. Note that he did not exercise his right to go further off by himself and mourn the loss of his cousin and precursor. When he saw the great crowd, "he had compassion for them and cured their sick" (Matthew 14:14). So, who did Jesus think he was? It is clear that he saw himself as the One who announces the reign of God. And his power, divine or otherwise, is to be exercised on behalf of God's people, not for his own benefit.

It seems clear that Jesus sees himself in a line with Moses and Elijah, both of whom had fed bread to the hungry. Together with Moses, "the Israelites ate manna forty years, until they came to a habitable land" (Exodus 16:35). And Elijah assured the widow who showed him hospitality with her last bit of flour and oil that "Thus says the Lord the God of Israel: The jar of meal will not be emptied and the jug of oil will not fail until the day that the Lord sends rain on the earth" (1 Kings 17:14). Both Moses and Elijah, however, required divine assistance to show beneficence. Jesus, of course, is divine assistance. He considers the young boy's offer of the five loaves and two fish and says, "Bring them here to me" (Matthew 14:18).

When he orders the crowds to sit down on the grass, he himself takes the bread and fish, looks up to heaven and prays a blessing. One imagines him saying to the Father, "Work with me here." He knows who he is; he operates out of love and prompted by compassion, but he, too, pauses and looks up. Jesus, himself both giver and gift, here reveals again his human identity and unfolding understanding of his relationship to the Father, a model for the spirituality of all who seek to work, pray, and abide with him.

Who Were the Disciples?

Consider next the disciples. As many miracles as they have witnessed, they never seem to anticipate the next one. As they come forward in procession through the huge crowd carrying the most meager of resources, they must have thought that they could hear the crowd grumble, "Well, just who do they think they are?" Perhaps the crowd did wonder or even grumble. It is awesome to consider those few humble disciples with a pitiful pile of bread and fish. Who did they think they were? Some would be quick to suggest that they were the first bishops and they must have known the dignity that belonged to them as a consequence of their office. But note that they were neither composing canons to legislate life in the crowd nor catechisms to define what they hoped and believed, nor were they sitting on thrones or designing cathedrals. At the moment, they were not even arguing about who was the greatest (Mark 9:34). Their greatness came simply because they did as they saw Jesus do. It seems that these disciples thought they were some folks doing what their friend asked on behalf of hungry people. Noble vocation that. Perhaps they were first moved by obedience or fear rather than compassion. But they did do as the Lord commanded and modeled. "And all ate and were filled; and they took up what was left over of the broken pieces, twelve baskets full" (Matthew 14:20). Matthew counts those who ate as "about five thousand men, besides women and children" (Matthew 14:21). (Goodness knows how many there really were if women and children were not counted!)

If even the disciples who lived and walked with Jesus seem to us a little slow on the uptake, perhaps we need to see that not so much as failure or inattention, but as gift to us. If there is room for them in the boat and at the helm, certainly there is room for us. And because we are numbered not just among those in the boat, but among the boat's crew as pastoral ministers, we are obliged to work diligently in developing a spirituality that will serve us as we serve our boatmates. So we who have been plunged into the baptismal waters need to ask ourselves again and again who we think we are. It is clear that the church thinks we are "God's holy people, set free from sin by baptism" (Blessing of the Water), and "a new creation…clothed…in Christ" (Clothing with a Baptismal Garment), as well as "children of the light" (Presentation of a Lighted Candle).

If that is who we are, then that is who Joan is. In that case, pastoral ministers need to mobilize resources and get busy, working as Jesus did to further the reign of God which is even now in our midst. Even if our resources are meager and our selves are unsure and our efforts humble, we know that we are doing what we are called to do and being who we are called to be. We are called to the confidence "that the one who began a good work among you will bring it to completion by the day of Jesus Christ" (Philippians 1:6).

We are confident that we are doing not the priest's work, the things the beleaguered pastor cannot get to, but our own duties among God's people. And our model is Mary, the Mother of God and Mother of the church. Mary spoke confidently to Gabriel, becoming the model of all who will place themselves in service to God by service to the body of Christ. Her response is the mantra of the pastoral minister: "Here am I, the servant of the Lord; let it be with me according to your word" (Luke 1:38).

It is actually abundantly clear who Joan ought to think she is. Her identity depends on her hope, which is inseparable from her identity as a Christian and as a minister. Perhaps Joan and the mother-in-law both need to hear again: "And not only that, but we also boast in our sufferings, knowing that suffering produces endurance, and endurance produces character, and character produces hope, and hope does not disappoint us, because God's love has been poured into our hearts through the Holy Spirit that has been given to us" (Romans 5:3–5).

So, just who do you think you are?

Next we will consider our ambitions as pastoral ministers and turn to Jesus in the gospels to discover whether that which we seek and the manner of our movements are both orthodox and worthy.

For Reflection and Discussion

- Has anyone ever questioned your ministry? What was your reaction?
- In what ways is Jesus a model of spirituality for you?

Who Is the Greatest?

*They had been discussing among themselves
on the way who was the greatest.*　　❧ MARK 9:34

Once we have a firmer, growing appreciation of and understanding of our own identities as ministers in the church, we then seek to "grow together in love," as the Second Eucharistic Prayer puts it. Timothy describes a bishop's life in a way that seems to elucidate the kind of character expected of all of us who seek to serve, and our aim must be to grow into that description. Timothy notes that whoever aspires to the office desires a noble task. That person must be above reproach, temperate, sensible, respectable, hospitable, an apt teacher, not a drunkard, not violent but gentle, not quarrelsome, and not a lover of money, must manage the household well, keeping children submissive and respectful in every way. He asks how those who do not know how to manage their own households can take care of God's church (1 Timothy 3:1–5).

St. John of Capistrano had a similar prescription which spoke to all called to God's table: "We must glow with the brightness that comes from the good example of praiseworthy and blameless lives. Our upright lives will make us like the salt of the earth, and our wisdom like the light of the world that brings light to others." John reminded clergy—and today we read his message as directed to all pastoral ministers—that though we dwell on earth and are bound by the necessities of nature, we are at the same time engaged in earnest communication with the angels in heaven so that we may be pleasing to God and learn better how to serve. The lives of pastoral workers, he concludes, must be an example to others, showing how we are to live in the house of the Lord.

Daunting task, that! Pastoral ministers are clearly called to lives of virtue, and such virtue is clearly countercultural. We learn from our eminent teacher, Jesus, who calls us salt of the earth and light of the world (Matthew 5:14). The first disciples are not always models of attentiveness for us, but their inattention sometimes calls us to a deeper awareness of our vocational call to pastoral ministry. As Mark tells it in his gospel, for example, Jesus simply could not get a hearing when it came to predicting his passion. He teaches about his impending suffering, death, and resurrection. No response. But, "then Peter took him aside and began to rebuke him" (Mark 8:32). Why? Doesn't say.

A chapter later, we encounter Jesus journeying through Galilee with his disciples. He is teaching them and tells them that "The Son of Man is to be handed over and they will kill him, and three days after his death he will rise" (Mark 9:31). But they didn't get it and for some reason were afraid to question him. Apparently they had not heeded the advice of their first-grade teachers, who, if those teachers went to the same teachers' college as did yours and mine, undoubtedly had said that there is no such thing as a stupid question. But the disciples did not heed the advice of their second-grade teachers either, who must have told them that the only stupid question is the one you do not ask. But they did not ask. Jesus knows to whom he speaks and what obstacles prevent their informed hearing, and he says no more.

Imagine: they walk with the Redeemer of all humankind who tells them of the mystery which would be the most momentous and significant of all moments since the creation and until the parousia. But they had different fish to fry.

Other Pressing Matters

They come then to Capernaum and inside whatever house they had been traveling to, Jesus asks what they had been arguing about on the way. They remain silent. Because "they had been discussing among themselves on the way who was the greatest" (Mark 9:34). Aha! They could pay no attention to his prophecy because there were other pressing matters at hand. Imagine! Which of them was the greatest? Hmmm…let's see. How many votes for a fisherman or a tax collector or a small-time farmer? How many votes for the Pantocrator, the Lord and master of all creation, the Eternal Word of God who was present at creation when the Spirit of God hovered over the deep, the Savior and Redeemer of all humankind, God from God, Light from Light, true God from true God, who is one in being with the Father? No contest. Seems the disciples, when they were stumped by the prophecy of the upcoming paschal mystery, should have asked, "Huh? What?"

Imagine their hubris. If we would have needed to tally the vote called for in the paragraph above, the results would have been unanimous. No doubt the disciples are happy to be unnamed in this particular gospel story because surely they must blush even in heaven's perfection whenever the tale is read. Jesus is far gentler with them than we might be. He knows human hearts and human frailty, and does not rebuke them—he does not ask them "Who do you think you are?"—but instead speaks gently to them of his hopes for who they will become. And we who reflect on these gospel moments are ourselves blessed in any number of ways. First, the gentleness that Jesus shows them will indubitably be the same gentleness shown to us. But we might also conclude that if these apostles and disciples, the first to have heard the Word and on whose apostolic witness the church is built, bumble so and still find a place in God's reign, surely then there is room for you and for me.

So who is the greatest? At this question, the ears of pastoral ministers should perk up and listen carefully. Or, better, attend as St. Benedict suggests as he begins the Prologue to his "Rule for Monasteries": "Listen carefully, my child, to your master's precepts, and incline the ear of your heart" (Proverbs 4:20). Paradoxically, those who aspire to greatness must not seek the head of the line, but instead seek to be both last and servant. Jesus places a child in their midst and decrees that whoever receives such a child in his name receives both him and the One who sent him. He does not point to the child with the assumption that everyone thinks that kids are cute. Children were regarded then as non-persons, perhaps because of high infant mortality and the uncertainty that they would live until they could be useful rather than expensive and demanding. Who knows? At any rate, they were vulnerable and powerless. It would seem sensible, given all this, that the child he placed in their midst was a girl. Vulnerable, powerless, and female. So true power and real greatness will be found by welcoming and by serving those who are poor, vulnerable, and powerless. Here is the beginning of the church's preferential option for the poor and oppressed. In fact, *The Church in the Modern World* (*Gaudium et Spes*) from the Second Vatican Council begins: "The joy and hope, the grief and anguish of the men of our time, especially those who are poor or afflicted in any way, are the joy and hope, the grief and anguish of the followers of Christ as well."

Still Too Distracted

Even if those first followers of Jesus suffered from sensory overload, one might think that when the third prediction of the passion came around in Mark's gospel, they would have been all ears. They go off to Jerusalem and Jesus takes the Twelve aside. "He began to tell them what was going to happen to him" (10:32). But the Zebedee boys, James and John, have an urgent request that seems to take precedence: "Grant that in your glory we may sit one at your right and the other at your left" (10:37). Wow! Place cards before the passion; the head of the table for me; first things and first people first.

Here comes the evangelical insight again: We are called from an individualistic piety to a communal understanding. If we hear the message as "Jesus and me" and not as "Jesus and us," we have missed the entire point. We have yet to hear the gospel. Here then is revealed one of the most important features of the pastoral minister's job description and vocational imperative: to help the church better hear the gospel call to conversion. We are called to "be doers of the word, and not merely hearers" (James 1:22). Let's go back to those words of

St. John of Capistrano, who, speaking of those called to ministry, comments that "by the brightness of their holiness they must bring light and serenity to all who gaze upon them. Their own lives should be an example to others, showing how they must live in the house of the Lord." Truly this daunting call and worthy task defines orthodox ambition for those pastoral ministers who attend to the voice of Jesus.

Will there be tensions and distractions brought about by ambition? Discouragement? Surely. But trusting in the mighty breath of God's good Spirit, we'll continue both onward and upward. And walking the Way, who is Jesus, will promote our development spiritually for ministry.

Next we will consider how the Spirit, being God, can work wherever, whenever, and in whomsoever divine pleasure decrees.

For Reflection and Discussion

- In what ways does Timothy's description of a bishop apply to you and your ministry?
- In what ways do you bring "light and serenity to all who gaze upon you"? What is your reaction to this challenge?

An Unrestricted Spirit

My lord Moses, stop them!   ✼ Numbers 11:29

The Lord came in a cloud to speak to Moses and impart the news that Moses' responsibilities were too much for one person to bear. God then took some of the spirit that was on Moses and bestowed it on seventy elders. The spirit came to rest on them, and they prophesied. The scriptural author tells us in the Book of Numbers that two of these elders, Eldad and Medad, were not at this particular gathering, but that their names had been on the list of those to be commissioned. So the spirit came on them too, and they also prophesied.

A young man comes then to Moses, upset and irritated. "My lord Moses, stop them!" he implores. Does he speak with the voice of Joan's mother-in-law or what? Moses tells the kid to get a grip on himself and says fervently, "Would that all the Lord's people were prophets! Would that the Lord might bestow his spirit on them all!" (Numbers 11:29).

It is clear to Moses that division of labor in the service of God's reign is a good plan. This empowerment by God's spirit is God's idea and God's initiative and God has carried it out. The fact that the Holy One failed to follow the rubrics that the young man thought necessary points out that the divine initiative and the divine plan do not depend on following human rules. God, being God, can work where and in whom and when divine pleasure decrees.

It is not only in the Hebrew Scriptures that we see humankind offering assistance and advice to God as if such help were necessary. In Mark's gospel, John comes to Jesus to report: "Teacher, we saw someone casting out demons in your name, and we tried to stop him, because he was not following us." Note that John does not want this fellow to stop because he is opposed to Jesus, because he serves another God, or is somehow unorthodox in what he believes. No, "We tried to stop him, because he was not following us." He was not following the disciples, but he was honoring the Word of God. Jesus speaks: "Do not stop him; for no one who does a deed of power in my name will be able soon afterward to speak evil of me." And not only that, but "Whoever is not against us is for us." Now those who consider it impossible for some Christians to gain heaven because they belong to the wrong denomination must attend to the voice of Jesus: "For truly I tell you, whoever gives you a cup of water to drink because you bear the name of Christ will by no means lose the reward" (Mark 9:41).

There is a great evangelical effort afoot in the United States, and part of that effort in some denominations is to send their members door to door in neighborhoods asking folks if they have a church home where they worship on Sundays. When the response is, "Yes, I do have a church home where I worship," the evangelist ought then to say, "How lovely for you. Let's pray for each other. Bye now." But if the response is instead a rebuke that someone cannot go to heaven through the Catholic church, or the Presbyterian or the Methodist churches, then one can be sure that the Spirit of God has left the building and this evangelical effort is flawed or fraudulent. Vatican Council II solved this problem for Catholic people in declaring that Protestant communions hold "salvific importance" for their members. This is an important acknowledgement that God can and indeed does work wherever it pleases the Spirit to do so, including outside both church and sacraments. So perhaps the would-be evangelist should then be told firmly, "Thank you for your concern about my soul. But I think I hear my mother (or the pope!) calling. Bye now." If the person persists in pointing to the futility of your life in your particular church, even Miss Manners would approve of the door's being shut firmly to protect oneself from such outrage. Discussion is often of no use in such a situation.

But it is not just in interdenominational dialogue that we sometimes run into rough spots. Sometimes within the church, member may indicate to member that her or his particular view of Catholicism is deficient. We have members who feel it their duty to tell other members that they must shape up and fly right, or at least fly as the critic determines the flight plan.

Room for Everyone

But one of the fine aspects of belonging to an ancient and universal body, which has been kissed by divinity and promised the continued guidance of God's good Spirit, is that age and size and Scripture and tradition all assert that there is room for everyone, and that, in fact, "In my Father's house there are many dwelling places" (John 14:2). James Joyce, considering the church in the last century, observed, "Here comes everybody."

Of course our efforts are flawed: we are flawed. But that's why we're called "practicing Catholics." We still are at work, trying always to get it right, trusting in God's transforming grace, hoping that we might be perfected "as your heavenly Father is perfect" (Matthew 5:48). Some will point out that the invitation of Jesus cautions, "Enter through the narrow gate; for the gate is wide and the road is easy that leads to destruction, and there are many who take it" (Matthew 7:13). But where is it written that any particular Catholic knows what for another is surely the road to destruction? We are bound, of course, to justice, and called to charity, but those who suggest that their narrow way is the will of Jesus and the only hope of the church ought to be suspect, and one might legitimately ask if they are themselves attentive to both justice and charity. The narrow gate seems to be the path of virtue. And those who are not virtuous, even if they are observant of the law, may find themselves surprised by the discussion at the throne of grace on the day of judgment. Jesus continues in Matthew to say that "the gate is narrow and the road is hard that leads to life," but also cautions, "Beware of false prophets, who come to you in sheep's clothing but inwardly are ravenous wolves. You will know them by their fruits. Are grapes gathered from thorns, or figs from thistles?" (7:14–16). Is this a call to kindness and to charity in our dealings one with another? It would certainly seem so.

It is grand to have a personal vision of one's responsibilities to the furthering of God's reign. If that call suggests that one should be transformed under the gospel and with the guidance of the church, who could argue that the call is from God? But if, instead, the call is to transform someone else's life and to have others conform to my own vision, the one so challenged may well indeed wonder if a false prophet has arisen. And such a bullying tactic seems to have provoked Jesus: "If any of you put a stumbling block before one of these little ones who believe in me, it would be better for you if a great millstone were hung around your neck and you were thrown into the sea" (Mark 9:42).

Those of us in pastoral ministry may sometimes feel that we know best. When we are so tempted, we need to refresh for ourselves our call to be one among God's holy people on pilgrimage from here to eternity. Our task is to be pilgrims and wayfarers and seekers together, serving not just as guides, but as companions. St. Augustine is our model here when he commented in the fourth century that "for you, I am a bishop. With you, I am a Christian." So we call to mind again our baptismal dignity, confident that set free from sin by baptism, we are a new creation clothed in Christ and children of the light. And let us remember that "God did not give us a spirit of cowardice, but rather a spirit of power and of love and of self-discipline" (2 Timothy 1:7).

This spirit, keeping the mystery and mission of Jesus alive in our midst, calls us to a life of justice and charity. To sin against either justice or charity is at least unwise. The absence of virtue is, of course, the path to destruction. But our call in Jesus is to newness and fullness of life. Life on that road is not only purer and sweeter, but a surer path to happiness.

Next we will consider why we should set our sights on Jesus and explore his teachings from a Christian perspective.

For Reflection and Discussion
- Do you experience in your ministry that you are a "pilgrim and a seeker" among other pilgrims and seekers? In what ways?
- What are your greatest obstacles to "newness and fullness of life" in your ministry?

Claiming a Path

You have become a new creation,
And have clothed yourself in Christ.
                         ✺ Rite of Baptism

Consider the case of classmates Spike and Ralph, together at a class reunion years after their high-school friendship lapsed. The reunion was a great opportunity for both to see old friends, former teachers, and classmates. As the party progressed, Spike suggested that a small group of them keep on carrying on, and move the party just down the block to his home. They did. Once there, Spike had one more drink. He didn't have to drive anywhere, so he drank perhaps more than would otherwise have been prudent. Ralph, a priest, knew what was coming. For priests and other pastoral ministers, this is an occupational hazard: Spike would want to talk theology or religious practice. (What's the deal with inebriates of the lapsed-Catholic persuasion anyway?)

As northern Minnesotans, they should have been talking sports or weather. Even in July, northern Minnesotans talk and dwell either on hockey or the unusually poor sledding weather. "I saw Coach Sertich in the Super Valu and he said to me…" they're supposed to say. Or, "Enough weather for you lately?" they're supposed to ask. It's in a northern Minnesotan's contract. Not Spike. It was quiet; an angel might have just passed through the room. Spike announced, after being certain that he had Ralph's attention, "I don't go to church anymore. Not ever. Not even Christmas or Easter." How is the pastoral minister supposed to respond? "Congratulations, Spike!" Or, "Your mother must be proud!" Or, "I'm not paid on commission anymore!"

This party-time dilemma is both a problem and an opportunity for pastoral ministers who in social settings and grocery stores and on soccer sidelines, will be asked to address dilemmas that confound God's people. The invitation extended in such settings is not really a call for your personal opinion about how to handle the difficulty, but a query about how the church addresses such issues. Here pastoral ministers are called to be gatekeepers of the church's treasury, looking to Scripture and ancient writers and ecclesial tradition to help explicate the mystery in which we live.

For example, the third-century document *Didascalia Apostolorum* addresses this problem, which has apparently plagued the church in every age. Maybe Ralph should have preached a couple of sentences from it: "Let no one diminish the ecclesia by his absence, that the body of Christ may not be diminished by one member. Do not tear apart the body of Christ!"

But Spike continued. "I may not go to church anymore, but I'll tell you this." Pause, two, three, four. "I am a very fine Christian. Very fine." Well, there is this stuff about pride and humility that he may have overlooked, but Ralph didn't mention it. It really wasn't Spike speaking, after all. It was instead the voice of their friend, Jack Daniels. But because pastors and pastoral workers are often much like the family doctor, perhaps Ralph should have said, "Take two aspirin and call me in the morning."

Spike is a good man. He loves his wife, Wanda. He cares about and for his family. He does not defraud anyone in his business. He may love Jesus. Jesus, no doubt, loves him. But it is dubious whether or not Spike can qualify as good Christian or good Catholic. This religious business is a social affair. It is not about someone at home in his Lazy-Boy recliner loving the Lord who (as "The Unsinkable Molly Brown" sings of her husband, Leadville Johnny Brown) loves "just to look at me."

When Spike and Ralph were high school frosh, Father Fred Fox (of happy memory), in Social Problems 101, told Spike that he would be just like his father in about fifteen years. Father Fred (may he be with God), rarely wrong, missed this call. Spike is, as Ralph observed, less a contributor to God's reign than was his father, whose strong presence and undying Catholic loyalty made the church a formative presence in Spike and Ralph's formative years. Spike is neither an envelope holder nor a contributor. There is no way it would be apparent that he is or ever was a Catholic were it not for his postprandial protestations. The church is smaller and poorer for Spike's absence.

A New Mission

If those who remain choose not to diminish or be diminished, the call to evangelism in this age must mean a new mission to the baptized who were not catechized, or were imperfectly catechized, or who somehow lost the way or the will. Instead of waiting for Spike to call, maybe Ralph should be in touch with him one morning soon, inviting him to come home with all his energy and critical insight. "Look homeward, angel," he could say. And, "You can come home again." They can stand together on the heights, in the valleys, and on the plains where God's breeze is sure to blow. They can transform the face of the earth. Here, then, is a vision of evangelization: calling ourselves and one another from an individualistic piety to a communal understanding. Understanding this truth is foundational to building and developing and growing in a spirituality as an ecclesial minister.

Spirituality is popular these days, and authentic Christian spirituality will promote renewed appreciation of gospel invitations and mandates. We must get ourselves and those to whom we minister into a communal mind-set so we can hear the gospel correctly. This is very difficult when almost everything in our culture is antagonistic to community. Our first impulse when we seek ministerial readiness may be to gather all the resources we can find, searching high and low and everywhere, and decree that everything that does not hurt us must make us better Christians. We will exhaust ourselves in that kind of search. The great St. Augustine, fourth-century bishop in North Africa and prodigious preacher and writer of theology, wrote in his

Confessions of yearning to see the face of God, asserting that his restless heart would find rest only in God.

We will come across some would-be guides who point to the yearning which is native to the human spirit and think that it can best be fulfilled by careful attention to native religions, to the Dalai Lama, to Hinduism and Buddhism and Islam and the mysticism of the Kabbalah. All of these traditions have elements of goodness, and we do not deny that they can be paths to truth and to God. But no one can walk all these paths. Simply to number them and learn some small piece of each would be a daunting task, and not necessarily illuminative of the path which is Christ. Developing a spirituality is different from developing multiple spiritualities, or a piecemeal spirituality, or a theory of spiritualities.

Christ at the Center

Some writers will assure us that the transformative presence of the divine was understood better by people in earlier ages than by moderns. They encourage us to watch and listen, which is good, but somehow seek to convince us that wisdom will be found best or most on the fringe or even outside of our Christian culture. We are called to remember the words of Jesus: "I am the way, and the truth, and the life. No one comes to the Father except through me" (John 14:6).

Some suggest, though perhaps incorrectly, that a chasm separates the natural and supernatural worlds and we need guides, preferably from other traditions, to cross the great divide. Writing in his very interesting *The Catholic Imagination*, Andrew Greeley suggests instead that ordinary Catholics tend to picture God, creation, the world, society, and themselves the way great artists do—as drenched with grace, with God's passionately forgiving love. God has created marvels great and small, and one of the gifts the Spirit gives is that of awe and wonder in the presence of these gifts.

We need not look then to other traditions to be more solidly Christian. Our own tradition contains wisdom that can enrich. There may be much to admire in an eclectic approach that seeks to cull insight into God's immanence in all or many of the world's traditions. But such eclecticism may not serve to promote holiness and steadfastness in the long run. We who, like St. Augustine, have a spiritual home and a vision of God's reign, will be best served by plumbing the depths of our own tradition rather than setting out as seekers with a boundless horizon and no particular notion of being at home. Christian spiritual writers in every age have centered their reflections in the teachings of Christ, and this is where we belong. They span decades, centuries, and millennia, and include the voices of the ancient fathers of the church, as well as those of modern artists, writers, saints, and teachers. We are called to search that tradition, finding gems that have been buried in tomes often untouched by modern seekers, gathering prayer prompts and wise insights. What we will find is but a fraction of what might be found, and our search will no doubt be neither comprehensive nor representative. Good! Maybe our gathered insights will prompt us to go again to the gospels and epistles, reading with newly opened eyes, growing in a developing spirituality for ministry that suits and serves us as we grow in grace.

As we begin the next chapter, we will consider the person and the challenges of Jesus and God's reign, and our place as disciples and pastoral ministers by him and in him in that reign.

For Reflection and Discussion

- What in your particular ministry is the greatest obstacle to community?
- In what ways do you continue to "plumb the depths" of your own tradition? What opportunities for this do you offer others?

PART TWO

Living the Life of Jesus

Jesus and the Reign of God

*Blest are your eyes because they see
and blest are your ears because they hear.
I assure you, many a prophet and many a saint
longed to see what you see but did not see it,
to hear what you hear but did not hear it.*
          ❧ MATTHEW 13:16–17

This Jesus whom we seek and serve, the one who prompts us and opens our eyes, is the object of more queries and studies and opinions and articles than any other figure in history. He lived before there was a daily newspaper, before the term media was coined, before MTV, before the cult of personality created *People* magazine. Yet no other character in modern times or in any other era has occasioned such comment and study. No one else has inspired as many imitators and admirers. Jesus, Son of God, love's saving presence among humankind, is, of course, the first model for pastoral ministry. Attentiveness to his invitations, demands, and commands is the foundation of a spirituality for pastoral ministry.

The church's life of prayer highlights what we believe about what he teaches. An old Christian maxim suggests *lex orandi, lex credendi*. That is to say that the law of prayer establishes the law of belief.

Wonder what the church teaches about something or someone? Look in the church's official prayer and see there the reflection of what the church believes. The church's belief is revealed in the words of its prayer. Consider the Christmas preface to the Eucharistic Prayer below. What words does it use to identify Jesus as the Savior of humankind, the focus of human hope?

> *Father, all powerful and ever living God,*
> *we do well always and everywhere to give you thanks*
> *through Jesus Christ our Lord.*
> *In the wonder of the Incarnation*
> *your eternal Word has brought to the eyes of faith*
> *a new and radiant vision of your glory.*
> *In him we see our God made visible*
> *and so are caught up in love of the God we cannot see.*
> *And so, with all the choirs of angels in heaven*
> *we proclaim your glory and join*
> *in their unending hymn of praise.*

Jesus of Nazareth was born into common people, and he lived thirty-three years among them. He preferred the company and causes of the poor and oppressed. The gospels assert that Jesus was born of the House of David. Oddly, the genealogy of Jesus found in the beginning of Matthew's gospel traces the lineage of Joseph, the husband of Mary. Thus the lineage is not really that of Jesus himself. Remember that Luke tells the story of Mary having been overshadowed by the Holy Spirit. She conceived while still a virgin. Jesus was conceived without sexual intercourse having taken place. The point of Matthew's genealogy then is not that Jesus is Joseph's son, but that he was born of a royal line, the House of David. Out of David's house was to come the Messiah, the Savior of all humankind.

This Savior loved humanity enough to come and dwell on earth. He came with a radical vision of life in and for the human community. His vision found roots in the great Hebrew prophets. He proposed a reversal of values and of fortunes so that the first would be last and the last would be first. He lived this vision on earth, and he challenged others to live as he did. Jesus called for a new humanity and a new earth. This challenge was at the heart of his preaching about the reign or the kingdom of God.

The Secret to Living

Jesus knew that not all would heed or live by his message. He said, "Let anyone with ears to hear listen!" (Mark 4:9). His call was to begin living differently, living morally, living righteously. Jesus knew the secret, and this secret was about how to live. Following him would be a guarantee that life would not remain an empty riddle, nor would life end on the day of death.

The secret was found in his life of compassion, in hearing others, attending to their distress. This compassion is key for those in pastoral ministry; when we see him exercise it, we are called to ponder and to imitate, thus conforming us to him, our will to his will. Jesus intimately knew God the Father, with whom he was one. His highest duty, like that of the prophets, was to preach about God's reign, and to share that reign and that goodness with all people. In his own love and unwearying compassion, he taught and still teaches others to live, insisting that selfishness and hate destroy, while love will build a new and lasting earth. For Jesus, this kind of religion made life real.

John the Baptist prepared the way for Jesus. John was much like the Hebrew prophets of the Old Testament, the Jewish Scriptures. John demanded obedience to God's commands, preached repentance, called people to abandon sin and death, and to cling to what is good and upright. The baptism John offered was a pledge of repentance, a promise of a world to be renewed. How were these faithful people to prepare for the coming of the Messiah? There was just one way: begin a new kind of life in which love rules. Social inequality and oppression must end. He said, "'Let the one with two coats give to the one who has none. The one who has food should do the same'" (Luke 3:11).

Luke the gospel writer saw John as the fulfillment of Isaiah's prophecy (see 7:10–14). And Jesus saw John as his forerunner. The kingdom of God was close. Justice would triumph.

At the baptism of Jesus by John, the voice of God is heard, proclaiming, "This is my beloved Son. My favor rests on him" (Matthew 3:17). Jesus called people to repentance. Matthew writes that "Jesus began to proclaim this theme: 'Reform your lives! The Kingdom of heaven is at hand'" (4:17). His message was a clear and simple invitation to transform a weary world by a strong and consistent application of the vision of love. Like John and the prophets before him, Jesus also was on the side of society's poor and oppressed. His faith and his hope, his model for life in the human community, was not simply the vision of a Utopia. His life and love would inaugurate God's reign.

The Reign of God

Christians, even pastoral ministers, have often misunderstood the notion of God's kingdom, thinking that it refers simply to heaven, a place or a state which is entered when life on earth is complete and one's body lies in the grave. Careful attention to the gospels suggests that this was not what Jesus preached. Salvation is not an individual's call but a social hope that involves all the community. God's radical intervention in the human community means that the earth is good, as is the human community that dwells here. "Radical," remember, refers to the roots, the original or fundamental meaning. Why is it that the earth and humankind are both good? "God looked at everything he had made, and he found it very good" (Genesis 1:31).

Jesus came to a confused earth, one steeped in sin and evil, and he offered the promise of redemption. Because extending that offer in the name of Jesus and the church is the business of pastoral ministers, we are called to pay particular attention when Jesus speaks of the kingdom of God, for he speaks of developing society and of popular hope. He does not speak of conquering by violence and war. In fact, after the vast crowd was fed with the multiplied loaves and fish, they were so impressed with the wisdom, ability, and compassion of Jesus that they wanted to make him their king. He withdrew. God's kingdom is not an earthly empire, and it will not be established by methods that appeal to the crowds. (See Matthew 14:22–23, John 6:14–15.)

In the desert, confronted by the tempter, Jesus would not call angels to deliver bread when he fasted. This was not how the Messiah's reign was to begin. John the Baptizer thought that the Messiah's reign would begin with judgment (see Matthew 3:10–12). Jesus said judgment would come at the end, the wheat with the weeds (see the story in Matthew 13:24–30).

"The soil produces of itself first the blade, then the ear, finally the ripe wheat in the ear" (Mark 4:28). Incidentally, you may have seen this Scripture quotation on the front page of *The Christian Science Monitor*. This fine newspaper points to much of what is good in human society. Looking for advancement in human ability to live together, it reports good news. Jesus was the best preacher of good news. He promised the final judgment in the future. But what was important in the present moment was the sowing of seed. How then would the kingdom come? Like a blast out of the blue? Asked by one of the Pharisees when God's reign would come, Jesus said: "You cannot tell by careful watching when the reign of God will come. Neither is it a matter of reporting that it is 'here' or 'there.' The reign of God is already in your midst" (Luke 17:20–21). "Let anyone with ears to hear listen!" (Luke 14:35).

The parables, the stories told by Jesus, provoke reflection and insight. The work of God is seen in beginnings. God is a crafter and lover of promise, but the finished product is a distant reality. The journey of life points to and promises future glory, but God is the pilgrim's guide and the pastoral minister's way, and it is in and on the journey that God's promise is revealed.

Jesus makes room at the table for all those who would come. Dining in the house of a leading Pharisee, Jesus sketched his vision of God's reign where all are welcome at the table. Another guest at the party delighted in this insight and exclaimed, "'Happy is the one who feasts in the kingdom of God'" (Luke 14:15). This insight in forever enshrined and celebrated in the Christian Eucharist. Before the faithful receive the Eucharist, the presider shows the consecrated bread and wine, and says, "This is the Lamb of God / who takes away the sins of the world. Happy are those who are called to his supper." Jesus makes it clear that old divisions between Jew and Gentile are beginning to fade. The new dividing line is between good and evil, between those with open hearts and good will and those with closed hands and selfish interests. Paul reflects this intent and dream of Jesus when he writes, "All of you who have been baptized into Christ have clothed yourselves with him. There does not exist among you Jew or Greek, slave or freeman, male or female. All are one in Christ Jesus" (Galatians 3:27–28). What kinds of changes might be in store if the church rereads and reconsiders this expression of Jesus' hopes? How do the lofty conceptions of the Savior challenge those who read them and try to follow today?

Remember that John, the forerunner of Jesus, boldly claimed that the kingdom of God was near. Jesus, on the other hand, taught that "the reign of God is already in your midst" (Luke 17:21). Who can enter? Those who experience metanoia, a change of mind, of heart, of attitude. Jesus warned that "I assure you, unless you change and become like little children, you will not enter the kingdom of God." These will be "of greatest importance in that heavenly reign" (Matthew 18:3–4).

The Vision of Jesus

This vision of Jesus, and the call of pastoral ministry, is to transform society, honoring the earth and its human inhabitants. The point is not so much to get individuals to heaven, but to change the disharmony of earth into the peace of God's reign. Jesus, human himself, knew and understood human nature, the social bent of humankind, the needs that call all people into community. His mission, then, was to prepare men and women to live together, promoting harmony and goodness. The fundamental virtue, of course, is love, for only love will build a better earth and will stimulate commitment to the common good.

All of this insight made Jesus a profoundly sociable companion. He would often engage others in conversation. Those with whom he conversed and those he chose as companions often shocked folks with a conventional sense of decency. He spoke with the Samaritan woman at the well, and even she was surprised: "You are a Jew. How can you ask me, a Samaritan and a woman, for a drink?" (John 4:8). Tax collectors, too, whom polite society regarded as no more than robbers, also came into the company of Jesus. He visited their homes and they ate together. Jesus made the meal a true social occasion, and those who would understand Jesus and his ways and the sacraments that evolved among his followers, must seek to understand the Jewish significance of table fellowship.

When contemporary preachers and theologians refer to the preferential option for the poor, they point back to Jesus's own preference for the poor. Here was the beginning of the fulfillment of his mother's song: "He has deposed the mighty from their thrones / and raised the lowly to high places. / The hungry he has given every good thing, / while the rich he has sent empty away" (Luke 1:52–53).

Jesus saw riches as a point of division in society. Those who are rich do not feel the same dependence on others as do the poor, nor do they necessarily feel the same kind of responsibility towards others as often the poor do. Such is both the blessing and the curse of riches. This is the dilemma of the rich young man who approaches Jesus. "What must I do to share in everlasting life?" he asks. Jesus answers that he ought to obey the commandments, and the youth answers, "I have kept all these since my childhood." Jesus looked at him with love and said, "There is one thing more that you must do. Go and sell what you have and give to the poor; you will then have treasure in heaven. After that, come and follow me." The young man went away sad, the gospel reports, because he had many possessions (Mark 10:17–22).

Jesus then observes that it is difficult for the rich to enter God's reign. In fact, "'it is easier for a camel to pass through a needle's eye than for a rich man to enter the kingdom of God'" (Mark 10:25). Some scholars or preachers will suggest an allegorization of what Jesus says, asserting that he referred to a rocky place which a camel could pass through only with difficulty. They seek to make a hard saying less hard. That does not seem to be the meaning in this gospel story, as Jesus asserts a bit later that "for God all things are possible" (Mark 10:27). There is a radicalism here that some try to spiritualize or soften, but it remains clear that the fundamental sympathies of Jesus were with the poor and oppressed. He helped them with his healing power, with heroic generosity and authentic compassion.

A Reversal of Fortunes

The Messiah's message was about reversal of fortunes: the poor would be fed, the rich sent away. Those to be blessed were those upon whom the world had not smiled. The bold Jesus suggested that each serve the other. Tyranny must be abandoned in favor of community. Greatness would be found when rank and honor, envy and anger were renounced. Who then is the greatest? Even the apostles quarreled about this, and at the Last Supper no less! Jesus reminded them that earthly kings lord their authority over their people. "But not so with you" (Luke 22:26). Here is the revolutionary Jesus pointing to a new world order, a new way of living together.

There is great power in the words of Jesus. If those who consider themselves his followers were to live in conformity to his words for a full day, the world as we know it would be launched into a new orbit. Even on the cross, Jesus did not abandon this vision, and his followers came to know that the suffering of the cross, which seemed utter folly, had beyond it resurrection, new life, a transformed earth, and the promise of the fullness of God's reign.

The faith of Jesus and the possibility of God's kingdom continue to quicken humanity's hope in the promise of peace, in the transformation of culture. Jesus was not merely a social reformer, not just a man who would have the earth be better. Instead, his vision was of a completely new order, and religion was at its heart. The new humanity which he envisioned and to which he called those who would follow is the promise of redemption that still beckons to humanity even today. Imagine an earth where people would dare to live the fullness of the message of Jesus! Issuing that invitation and fueling the dream is the stuff of pastoral ministry.

Jesus knew that his message was explosive, and that those who would hear and follow would not be silent. In fact, he was told during his entry into Jerusalem that he should rebuke his disciples. Apparently they were too loud and embarrassed the more sedate and orderly city residents. The entire crowd of disciples was shouting "'Blessed is he who comes / in the name of the Lord! / Peace in heaven and glory in the highest'" (Luke 19:38–39). The complainers did not associate this cry with the very similar message of the angels to the shepherds earlier in Luke after the birth of the infant (2:14). Jesus, of course, made the connection, and he told the Pharisees who would have the disciples be still that "'If they were to keep silence, I tell you the very stones would cry out'" (19:40). Their cry would be in joy at the presence of the one in whom all the earth will find salvation. We who seek peace, who seek a growing spirituality to guide our lives and ministry, will continue to return to the gospels as the focus of our imitation of Jesus. When we seek to conform our lives to his, we are on the true spiritual path.

Next I will offer a brief personal reflection about the importance of both imagination and hope in our ministry.

For Reflection and Discussion

- In what ways are you a sign of compassion for others in your ministry?
- How do you experience the "reign of God already in your midst"? How do you help make it known?

Imagination and Hope

As I turn and return to the Jesus of the gospels, I bring my own story and history, as do we all. I often recall that there were two kinds of wishes in our home when we five kids were growing up, and memory of them guides my way in ministry. Only one of those ways of wishful thinking was encouraged. We might say, for example, that we would like to flap our arms and fly to the moon. That flight of fancy would be encouraged. We might be asked by the adults in the extended family to provide details, to expand the idea into a more complete story. These other lives within a story were encouraged particularly by our father who, on those nights when he put us to bed, would gather us into one of the big beds and continue the never-ending story of an imaginary rabbit family (based on the story of Peter Rabbit). Dad invented the rest of the rabbit family and other creatures of the forest, and he continued night by night to weave the intricate tales of the rabbits and their adventures. This kind of fanciful, wishful thinking became a sacred, peaceful activity. These were delicious holy moments.

Another kind of wishful thinking was not encouraged in our home. "I wish my arithmetic were done and I could watch television," for example. The child who said that to a parent or aunt or uncle would expect to see upturned eyeballs and hear the adult say, "I wish I were lying down." That was an inside family joke. We talked in a code sometimes, and that one sentence reminded us of an antique incident we considered quite funny in a pathetic sort of way, but a story that also reminded us to do what needed to be done.

Grandma Graham, who died before my parents were married, is said to have told of a woman in bed, propped up on pillows. "I wish I were lying down," the woman said. We were told about this woman and her extraordinarily lazy wish on countless occasions. "Why didn't she just lie down then?" we would always ask. Aunt June would laugh, sigh, "Oh, honey!" and caress the child's cheek, but never answer the question. Mother, however, might patiently attempt to explain what was really very obvious.

I have never forgotten about this woman propped up on pillows who wished she were lying down. I have always been able to imagine the woman and even the bed and the pillows, and an open book on her lap and a box of chocolates to one side. And she wished she were lying down. I don't know if this woman ever lived and was a friend or acquaintance of Grandma's. Somehow, that didn't matter. She has always been as real to me as any inhabitant of my town.

Still today in my family, any wish that shouldn't be a wish but should instead be a call to action is met by an understanding but unsympathetic look and the simple statement, "I wish I were lying down." That reminder is given freely across generational lines: to the sister who wishes that the company car could be a BMW and not a Civic, to the cousin who would like to be a doctor but can't quite seem to finish the first year of college, to the priest who wishes that all the summer weddings could be performed in one huge ceremony so that the summer evenings could be freed up for other, less noble activities.

I have only recently understood that gentle voices of pastoral authority are, in fact, the voice of the Holy Spirit. The Spirit moves among us to cure us. The Spirit, too, helps us to rejoice. He quickens us with hope. We are advised in the First Letter of Peter: "Should anyone ask you the reason for this hope of yours, be ever ready to reply, but speak gently and respectfully" (1 Peter 3:15–16) Our hope is that Jesus promises us this Spirit. I am glad when I recognize his presence.

I brought all of these reflections to a graveside on a recent Saturday afternoon when we buried my twenty-two-year-old cousin. Jonathan was named for his Uncle John, who was my father. We buried Jonathan in a grave at Forest Lawn near Grandma Graham, who first told the story of the woman who wished she were lying down. Jonathan's hopes have been left unfulfilled, his family left in shock and grief. His wishes, whatever they were, will not be met on this earth.

We who are in ministry must, together with those who survive, examine all our wishes, searching for the difference between fantasy and possibility. What we wish to do and what can be done, we must work to accomplish. It is in this that we build up our human community and give glory to God. God blesses this honest activity of ours; being about that activity and reflecting on it will ensure that we are on the road to building a spirituality that will continue to guide and shape us. We who love Jesus will go about these duties in love, and with both imagination and hope.

Next we will consider the importance of being sensitive to the "least ones" in our society—guided by Jesus and the church.

For Reflection and Discussion

- How would you explain the difference between wishful thinking and hope?
- What is your fondest hope for the church and your ministry within it?

Sensitivity to the Poor

Spirituality is a process of being conformed
To the image of Christ
For the sake of others.
                   ❧ Robert M. Mulholland Jr.

I had not thought that one of the finest examples of pastoral sensitivity I'd encounter in Chicago would be in a classroom full of cops working toward their baccalaureate degrees. But that's where I found him: in a classroom at the Police Academy where we worked together to consider the place of Christian Social Thought in the lives of individual Christians, in the body of Christ, and in Chicago. This group of students considered the proposal that direct involvement with the poor, among other things, ought to make us cry out to God ever more urgently to show mercy to the oppressed by changing the hearts of their oppressors.

One of the students, a Windy City police officer with over two decades of experience on the force, wondered aloud why we would pray "for those pieces of s***?!" He was challenged by the professor and the other students to answer the question himself. He actually did so remarkably well, beginning by tracing the path of his recent classwork. His effort is of special note to pastoral ministers in that he made careful use of both scripture and church documents in answering the question, crafting his own developing opinion in light of those sources.

He immediately put aside his initial vulgarism, and began with *Gaudium et Spes,* The Pastoral Constitution on the Church in the Modern World, which insists that the human person has sublime dignity. He noted that the adjective sublime, which finds its roots in the Latin for "high, or elevated," means 1) lofty, grand, or exalted in thought, expression, or manner, or 2) of outstanding spiritual, intellectual, or moral worth, and 3) tending to inspire awe usually because of elevated quality (as of beauty, nobility, or grandeur) or transcendent excellence. If God has given that awesome dignity to humankind, it has been given to each man and woman. No one is left out. Though some may choose to act in ways that seem not in keeping with their sublime dignity, the dignity is there by virtue of birth. Leo XIII noted in *Rerum Novarum* that the state cannot take away rights that humans have had since before the state existed. If states cannot take away one's human rights, then one individual may not take away another's rights either, including human dignity and the respect that such dignity commands. God's gift of dignity, which can be squandered, must not be disrespected by any individual.

Inspired by the Bible

"But where did the fathers of Vatican II find their inspiration to craft such a document?" classmates asked in follow-up. "Were the bishop-writers pointy-hatted intellectuals or vestment-clad children of the sixties? Were their dogmatic assertions born in that moment, or of reliable roots?" On a roll, the officer paused, flipped open his Bible, and made specific reference to the creation story in which God decides to make humankind in the divine image, after which, God saw every created thing, "and indeed, it was very good" (Genesis 1:31). Not yet ready to stop, he moved on to Psalm 8, in which David lauds God for having made humans "a little lower than God, and crowned them with glory and honor. / You have given them dominion over the works of your hands; you have put all things under their feet" (Psalm 8:5–6). Who can disrespect such a creation?

How do hearts become hardened and how does one become an oppressor, and why? Who knows? But such hardness is an abomination in the eyes of God, he asserted, pointing next to Psalm 95 in which God warns, "Do not harden your hearts." Those "whose hearts go astray," and who do not regard God's ways are to hear the warning: "They shall not enter my rest" (Psalm 95:8, 10–11). Christian charity calls the prayerful, suggested the officer, to pray for those whose hearts are hard, asking that hearts of stone be changed by God's grace into hearts of flesh. Only then can the world as it is be transformed into the fullness of God's reign; thus there is urgency to the task and to the prayer; we cannot delay even an hour or a day.

And all of these scriptural considerations, he asserted, had to be the inspiration of the great Jesuit poet, Gerard Manley Hopkins, when he wrote of the just one, who "Acts in God's eye what in God's eye he is— / Christ—for Christ plays in ten thousand places, / Lovely in limbs, and lovely in eyes not his…."

With such an attitude both in prayer and in good works, the officer said, overwhelming problems will seem more approachable. We will be quickened both in hope and in perseverance to work for a transformed society. And this, he concluded, is both our role and our duty as members of the body of Christ. One cannot argue with such airtight logic or so inspired a presentation. This kind of sensitivity and insight, as well as attention to the rich resources that guide our development, it seems to me, is the true school of a spirituality for ministry. Onward then and upward, with "Officer Insight" as companion and guide.

Next we will consider how we might assist others in making difficult choices in a way that also promotes growth in our own spirituality.

For Reflection and Discussion

- How would you (do you) explain to others the church's ministry to the poor?
- In what particular ways are you called upon in your ministry to give witness to Christ's love for the poor?

Gestures of Compassion

*Listen carefully, my child,
to your master's precepts,
and incline the ear of your heart.*
                 ❧ St. Benedict in the Prologue
                      to his Rule for Monasteries

How is it possible that a college student who cannot see the value of a research assignment nor find two sources to substantiate a scholarly point he wishes to make, can, while suffering shock and stress, locate an abortion clinic in a distant city, make an appointment for his girlfriend, and find the funds necessary to pay for the procedure all in the space of a few hours? His prowess in that particular piece of research might cause heads to spin. But such a soul, old enough to produce sperm and impregnate a willing partner, wily enough to research how to end an unwanted pregnancy, is not always wise enough to consider all of the ramifications of his and their act, and will seek out pastoral counseling in odd but unthreatening venues. Paying attention to his query and his pain will serve him well, but will also school the pastoral minister in continuing to craft a spirituality for ministry.

"May I ask you a personal question?" he might ask upon spying you in the grocery store or college stairwell or corridor to the restrooms in a pizza parlor. You might anticipate his asking if all that hair is really yours, how someone so tall rides in a compact car, or if you prefer the

White Sox over the Yankees. But he might instead well ask, "What do Christian people think about abortion?" When he does, know that his is not an idle question. He is neither asking a historical question, nor inquiring about comparative morality among denominations. He does not want an academic answer, "Well, the Catholic church teaches…but some Protestant groups…while other individuals in good conscience…." Nor is he asking your opinion, what you might do if confronted by an unwanted pregnancy while unmarried, not in love, poor, frightened, and pressed for time. Here is an opportunity to provide information, compassion, direction, and pastoral care.

"Do you mean, what does the Catholic church teach about what we might do when surprised by an unwanted pregnancy?" you could ask in return. You'll know immediately if the question hits home.

Many pastoral ministers will suggest that Catholic teaching on abortion is so clear that it really need not be spoken of often. Statistics, however, suggest that Catholic youth are not much different from Protestants or the unchurched with regard to procuring abortions. Those who ask what the teaching is may well be asking just that, and, in addition, may be asking to talk about being in a difficult situation where not all options are immediately clear.

"Do you know that the church imposes a penalty on those who have abortions, as well as on those who assist them in procuring abortions?" you might ask at some point in the conversation (but surely this is not the place to begin). The penalty, excommunication, is serious and severe, and indicates the attention with which the issue is to be approached. Some in such a stressful situation find that their logic also suffers from stress, and they propose for themselves remedies that will not stand up to careful scrutiny. "We do not think we are able to raise a child, but also do not feel that it would be right to have our child raised by someone else." There is the limping logic: It would be hard or maybe impossible for us to raise a child, but rather than giving that gift to another, we feel the life should be snuffed out. Some will suggest that the woman has a right to control her body, overlooking the fact that some mutual sense of self-control might have prevented the unwanted pregnancy. Others might assert that since the church is not in favor of artificial means of birth control, pregnancy outside of marriage is the logical outcome. They forget that premarital, genital sexual activity has not been regarded as virtuous by the church in any age.

More Discernment Needed

"We are not ready to commit ourselves to each other in marriage" is an admission better made before marriage than in a divorce court or marriage tribunal. "We are not willing to give up all that we would have to give up to be responsible, loving parents" could be the beginning of mature discernment.

Young adults who can research paths to the abortion clinic in record time are also capable of discovering alternative plans that respect the rights not just of the pregnant woman and her partner, but also of the developing life. Those who ask what the church teaches want to know, but they want and need to be informed gently, in such a way that invites their participation in life-giving and life-affirming strategies. They neither want nor need to be chided, to be quizzed on how such an event could have taken place, or asked why they did not take precautions once they had decided to become intimate. It will not profit them to be asked, nor you to ask, how they could not have known that the back seats in today's Chevy Blazers can be just as dangerous as the Nash Ramblers of old.

Here is the task for the pastoral minister: to suggest, to console, to sympathize and empathize, to pray, to smile, to help, not ruling but guiding. Sometimes you can help; sometimes your gentle touch will make all the difference; sometimes you can be light and wisdom to those who search in darkness. Sometimes you cannot do these things, and you go home burdened by what might have been. While your moments of judgment, irritability, and haste may live shamefully in your memory and in theirs, your gestures of love and compassion will never be lost or wasted.

"We've decided that our first choice was not our best plan," you may hear when next happening upon your interlocutor. Your initial meeting, more than a bump in a corridor, may have been an accidental grace as well as another step in the formation of a spirituality for ministry.

Next we will consider the importance of prayer in our ministry, especially the importance of praying as Jesus taught.

For Reflection and Discussion

- Do you encounter people in your ministry who believe "conveniently"? How do you share church teaching in such cases?
- In what ways do you share "accidental grace" through your ministerial encounters?

PART THREE

The Life of Prayer

What We Dare to Say!

*There is a general rule concerning all special graces
granted to any human being.
Whenever the divine favor chooses someone to receive a
special grace,
or to accept a lofty vocation,
God adorns the person with all the gifts of the Spirit
needed to fulfill the task at hand.*
        ※ From a sermon by St. Bernadine of Sienna

Central to a life in ministry is a life of prayer. In fact, ministry can only flow out of our prayer. Those who minister but cease to pray will first find themselves hollow, and usually, their ministry will seem unrewarding or futile, and then they will cease to minister (even if they remain employed in a ministerial capacity). Consequently, attention to our life of prayer is foundational both to life in Christ and to life in ministry.

Central to the prayer life of Christians is the prayer that Jesus gave us. In Luke 11, the disciples seem either unhappy or perplexed that John's disciples have been taught to pray, but their master has not taught them. They approach Jesus as "he was praying in a certain place, and after he had finished, one of his disciples said to him,

'Lord, teach us to pray, as John taught his disciples'" (Luke 11:1). Jesus neither reproaches nor offers recrimination, but gives them the prayer that seems prophetic with regard to message, mission, method, and attitude. Too often, we Christians seem to think that Jesus left the complete handbook for the operation of a church, including all necessary dogmas as well as the floor plan for Winchester Cathedral. It sometimes comes as a surprise that he who tells us "Do this in remembrance of me" (Luke 22:19) did not leave a prayer book, and the New Testament was not yet written as he spoke the command.

The fact that what we call the Lord's Prayer really is unique in all the world is a fact that ought not to be lost on us, and one we ought to remember as we continue the ancient tradition of reciting that prayer three times daily. It truly is the perfect prayer for morning, noon, and night, before and after meals, alone, or in good company, whenever and wherever Christians gather. But perhaps we are too blithe in saying these words. Annie Dillard suggests that we worshipers are not very sensible. She asks, "Does anyone have the foggiest idea what sort of power we so blithely invoke?" Perhaps crash helmets ought to be the order of the day. And "ushers should issue life preservers and signal flares; they should lash us to our pews." Such is the power of the God we invoke who "may draw us out to where we can never return." We ought, indeed, to be very careful in claiming in prayer the words Our Savior gave us.

God as Father

Jesus said to his disciples, "When you pray, say: Father, hallowed be your name" (Luke 11:2). For Jesus to call God Father or Abba was daring in its informality. God becomes accessible in a new and personal way, and God's love is revealed as unconditional. When we dare to call God "Father," we open ourselves to this relationship which really does extend to us. We embrace the good news that in Jesus we are offered divine life. God is now Father to us; we accept the gift of becoming God's children.

In his nineteenth-century paraphrase of Psalm 102, hymn-writer Henry F. Lyte wrote, "Father-like he tends and spares us; Well our feeble frame he knows; In his hands he gently bears us, Rescues us from all our foes. Alleluia! Alleluia! Widely yet his mercy flows." This is the God who is "Slow to chide, and swift to bless," and "Glorious is his faithfulness." We may sense an even deeper, more radical claim in Jesus' use, and our own, of Abba, and a broader, more inclusive sense of God. We have to dare to say it, to call on God as if we were children in the night. We must be "formed by the Word" before we really express this relationship and claim it boldly.

The notion of addressing God as Father is problematic for some modern Christians, and addressing this issue is inescapable for those in ministry. How we approach it flows from and shapes our spirituality. Ours is an inclusive age, and to use male titles for God evokes the image of a patriarchal church which is unsettling to many. If Jesus had some other form of address for God, the evangelists seem not to have recorded it. While feminists are helping us learn to read and reread the Scriptures in ways that will help us focus on what may have been lost, overlooked, or even suppressed, we have yet to make complete peace with the images of Father and Abba. They are incomplete. God is not a guy. But all images are incomplete, and only the God in whose presence we stand is perfect. All our attempts to imagine this God are flawed and will be flawed until we come to stand finally before the throne of grace (Hebrews 4:16). Those who have not known a dad's tenderness may also have trouble with the image of God as father. But the richness of the image, though incomplete and imperfect, teaches us that God is not just creator or redeemer or sanctifier or judge, but fatherly in expressing and acting on loving concern.

As our language continues to evolve, many struggle with translations that change Father to Creator. That change seems to lose or confuse the dimension of divine identity. The gender problem is part of the issue, reflecting an older understanding of biology which saw the father transmitting genetic identity to the child with the mother as receptor, nurturing the person begotten by the father. Some then call on God as Father and Mother. Pope John Paul I said, "God is

Father, yes. But even more, she is Mother." Some use the title parent because it is inclusive of both genders, but it seems to suffer a certain loss of warmth. To say simply Creator or Holy One invokes awe, but not a familial familiarity. The key is that God extends divine identity to us. The challenge is not to let the very real issues of language and gender keep us from the identity that belongs to us as baptized children of the most high God. We dare to claim the relationship which Jesus models and to which he invites us. To many, this may seem threatening or even blasphemous. In practice, we run the risk of continuing to ignore the implications of the gift, living our Christian lives as fearful servants on trial, hoping to go to heaven, but seeing earth as only a vestibule and not the theater of God's action and active love that it truly is.

As we move forward in pilgrimage, Jesus tells us to pray, "Your kingdom come" (Luke 11:2). Kingdom, too, is an unsettling word for many in our age. Some see it as another patriarchal reference. That unfortunate connotation is one of the reasons that God's reign is perhaps a better term for us than God's kingdom. Another reason is that kingdoms are bounded by time and space. Queen Elizabeth's kingdom (and why hers is not a queendom is a good question) is firmly situated where it can be seen, found, and landed upon. God's reign, on the other hand, is more about a way of living together in peace and unity, justice and love, than it is about geography or real estate. We are to remember that "Once Jesus was asked by the Pharisees when the reign of God was coming, and he answered, 'The reign of God is not coming with things that can be observed; nor will they say, "Look, here it is!" or "There it is!" For, in fact, the reign of God is among you'" (Luke 17:20–21). We were initiated into that reign when plunged into the saving waters of baptism. While it will come to fulfillment in heaven, it is not something unknown or foreign to us now.

Our Jewish brothers and sisters assert that if all of them, for just one day, were to keep the entire Torah, all of the law, the Messiah would come. Similarly, we Christians know that if we could live all of the gospel invitations and commands for a single day, the earth would be transformed, and we with it; the Messiah would come again in glory;

and, heaven would be wedded to earth. So each act and thought and word of ours is important, either by advancing the coming reign of God, or impeding its arrival by our sin and selfishness. We flawed keepers of both old and new covenants have not yet responded completely to God's call. We continue to move on, sinning and repenting, hoping one day finally to be perfected "as your heavenly Father is perfect" (Matthew 5:48).

Dependence on God

We ask next, "Give us each day our daily bread" (Luke 11:3). Note that we do not ask that our Franklin Funds or the Dow Jones continue to rise that we might accumulate huge piles of interest and retire finally in the style to which we hope to become accustomed. Instead, we pray to have an acute realization of our dependence on God, and that we might submit in faith to that dependency. This is the same notion of Islam, or submission, that Muslims hold. Together, we know that God is all powerful, and we creatures are dependent. We ask to be sustained with what we truly need, rather than with the fullness of all for which we ask.

In praying for forgiveness, we are truly bold. And we put ourselves at risk if we make this prayer carelessly. We say, "And forgive us our sins, for we ourselves forgive everyone indebted to us. And do not bring us to the time of trial" (Luke 11:4). Imagine that! We ask to be forgiven in the same way that we have forgiven others. We will certainly want to enjoy all the tenderness and loving kindness that the forgiving God has to offer. This insight will give new depths of meaning to Luke 6:30–31: "Give to everyone who begs from you; and if anyone takes away your goods, do not ask for them again. Do to others as you would have them do to you." And to Luke 6:35–38: "But love your enemies, do good, and lend, expecting nothing in return. Your reward will be great, and you will be children of the Most High; for he is kind to the ungrateful and the wicked. Be merciful, just as your Father is merciful. Do not judge, and you will not be judged; do not condemn, and you will not be condemned. Forgive, and you will be forgiven; give, and it will be given to you. A good measure, pressed down, shaken together, running over, will be put into your lap; for the measure you give will be the measure you get back."

Scripture does not tell us that the Lord's prayer concludes with "For the kingdom, the power, and the glory are yours," but that line is not the Protestant innovation many assume it to be. In fact, the *Didache*, or "Teaching of the Twelve Apostles," a second-century church document, records the line as early as AD 102 or 112. And even then, it was probably not an innovation but reflected the practice of the church.

Many people find theology and spiritual reading difficult. Theological words have come unmoored as people lose touch with the systems of thought that fit a previous age. Religious truths require context and coherency. Language needs revitalization. Familiar truths must be expressed in startling ways with an honesty about doubt that will force us to go deeper and further. We require that kind of originality all the more when the subject is as familiar as the Lord's Prayer. As we reconsider the current and coming reign of God and our place in it, and as we continue to make the Lord's Prayer our own, we might do well to remember and restore the invitation to that prayer from the liturgy before Vatican II: "Taught by Our Savior's command, and formed by the Word of God, we dare to say…." This prayer will draw us into something bigger than ourselves, richer than we can imagine, more terrifying in its demands than at first we knew. When we can sense that we are being drawn in, then the spirituality we have labored to develop will bear tasty and tangible fruit.

Next we will consider intercessory prayer, asking God, the one who shapes our spirituality, to be attentive to our every request and but to grant us that which we truly need.

For Reflection and Discussion

- How do you through your ministry offer "context and coherency" to the teachings of the church?
- In what ways is the Lord's Prayer a model for your own ministry? Which part of it best motivates you in your works?

Intercessory Prayer

*From his fullness we have all received,
grace upon grace.*   ❧ JOHN 1:16

I recently received an e-mail from a young man whom I had known when he was a college student some years ago. His update could be the first line of a country western ballad: "Hoboken didn't work out for me." He and his girlfriend spent three years near Hudson and First (close to the Path train to midtown Manhattan), but "Unfortunately, we split apart two months ago and went our separate ways." His high-tech job shut down and he moved back in with his parents and is currently selling vitamins and skin creams. He reports being confused about "why all this occurred" and is "trying to figure out the reason." He concluded the note with a plea commonly heard by Christians and most especially by those in ministry: "Say a prayer for me, would ya? I could use it."

The human heart feels itself pulled spontaneously to praise and thanksgiving, yet reaction to human need prompts many prayers in the form of petitions for favor, seeking God's intervention in both mundane affairs and those matters perceived to be of life-and-death significance. As we shape our spirituality for ministry, we consider the needs of those who have "left Hoboken" and all of those who ask us to assist them by our prayer.

The *Catechism of the Catholic Church* asserts that "transformation of the praying heart is the first response to our petition" (2739). And, "since the heart of the Son seeks only what pleases the Father, how could the prayer of the children of adoption be centered on the gifts rather than the giver?" (2740).

A condition of the efficacy of prayer is that it be "resolutely united with that of Jesus" and then "we obtain all that we ask in his name" (2741). The Catechism reader is reminded that "if we enter into the desire" of the Spirit of God, "we shall be heard." But two cautions are given, the first from Evagrius Ponticus: "Do not be troubled if you do not immediately receive from God what you ask him; for he desires to do something even greater for you, while you cling to him in prayer." And from St. Augustine: "God wills that our desire should be exercised in prayer, that we may be able to receive what he is prepared to give" (2737).

But are these prayers heard? The Catechism admonishes the questioner: "We ought to be astonished by this fact: When we praise God or give him thanks for his benefits in general, we are not particularly concerned whether our prayer is acceptable to him." However, "we demand to see the results of our petitions" (2735).

The Catechism seems to concur with Karl Rahner, who writes in his essay "On Prayer" that "of all types of prayer, the one which is most often arraigned before the bar of human judgment is the prayer of petition." He points out, in fact, that "the poverty and misfortune of the vast majority of mankind qualify them to enter the witness stand in the case against the worth of prayers of petition." He points to "the unheard prayers of children dying from starvation," and of "exploited slaves and betrayed women," and "of those crushed by injustice." Rahner points to the wonderment of those in pain who philosophize about God's remoteness; he asks if the one who "set this clockwork world spinning with the utmost accuracy" is "now unaware even of its humming."

But Rahner acknowledges that we nevertheless continue to turn to God, lifting our pleading hands in prayer, cherishing "a profound faith which cannot be shaken, despite endless disappointments." He suggests, "We must renew our faith in such prayer, and uphold its vital necessity." After all, "we know we are suspended over the abyss of our nothingness by a thread of the mercy of God, and that we cling to that mercy."

A Kind of Selfish Prayer

Rahner points out that we who can be unmoved by the misfortunes of others cry out when disaster hits us. When "our little nest of content is shaken by rough winds," we expect the blissfully ignored kingdom of heaven "to be immediately concerned with setting things right again for us, in order that we may be again in the 'happy' state of having no need of God." This is because "we have not grasped that the glory of God in this world is the Cross of his Son." We miss the point that we suffer because we sin. The evils from which we pray to be delivered, however, may not be evil at all when measured by God's standards. In fact, perhaps our prayer is not "a genuine lifting of our real or imagined sorrows to God, but just a selfish whine to have things adjusted our way." Such prayer, which really seeks to press our wishes on God rather than abandon ourselves to his will, "is not a prayer but an act of arrogance and rebellion."

But this is not to suggest that prayers of supplication are to be forsaken because Christ taught us how to pray, and until the parousia, "We have Christ as our answer to all accusations against prayer." It is Christ who teaches us to pray in supplication, confidence, and submission. Christ promises that all true prayer will be heard "to the extent to which we identify our will with that of the Father."

Cardinal John Henry Newman points out in a sermon entitled "Nature and Grace," that "salvation is not so easy a matter or so cheap a possession as we are apt to suppose. It is not obtained by mere wishing." So, the one who prays in faith returns with a deepened awareness to the formulation of the Catechism, understanding that the first fruit of prayer is the transformation of the heart of the one who prays. Gifts may be given; healings may occur. God the all-powerful can and does work wonders in every age. But perhaps no wonder is so great as the transformation of the human heart from stone to flesh, pliant in awe before God's design, compliant with God's good will, eager to see how God's goodness and tender mercy will allow both saints and sinners to cope with life's trials, confident that God does not abandon those who cry out, but is attentive in loving kindness. This is, I think, the reason that my young friend from Hoboken reaches out: he yearns for the transformation that prayer brings.

> *Next, let us consider the Eucharist, our food for the journey, the table which is the focus and the cause of the church's unity and our sure path to a better developed spirituality for ministry.*

For Reflection and Discussion

- In what ways does your ministry give witness to "a profound faith which cannot be shaken, despite endless disappointments"?
- How do you react to Cardinal Newman's phrase: "Salvation is not so easy a matter or so cheap a possession as we are apt to suppose"?

The Eucharist and Our Ministry

You have given us bread from heaven, containing within it all sweetness.

If prayer is the center of life and ministry, those who seek to develop a spirituality to feed and sustain that life will certainly see the Eucharist as central. Pondering the mystery of the Eucharist flows naturally from celebrating it, feeds the life of faith, and is a sure path to a rich spirituality for ministry.

When Moses wandered in the desert with the Israelites on their long journey to the Promised Land, he told the people to remember that God tested them by affliction. They would discover that in the midst of that affliction, God would not abandon them. God fed them with manna, bread from heaven. The connection between manna and the Christian Eucharist ought to be obvious. We, too, are fed with bread from heaven, bread containing within it all sweetness. When Catholics still prayed in Latin, they would chant this truth during Benediction of the Blessed Sacrament. The priest would intone, "you have given us bread from heaven." The people would respond, "containing within it all sweetness." Just as those bowed in prayer remembered and gave thanks, so also are Christians who gather at the eucharistic table today to remember and give thanks for the signs of God's providence.

The book of Deuteronomy makes an important point in this regard. This fifth book of the Bible first spoke to our brothers and sisters who share the faith of Abraham and Sarah. Consider the story you see in 8:2–3, 14–16. Together, both Jews and Christians are reminded that God is always faithful. In the body and blood of Christ, Christians are given the new and unending sign of God's never-diminishing care. Every celebration of the Eucharist brings all past signs of God's love to the present moment.

The Christian Eucharist

The Apostle Paul's first letter to the church at Corinth contains one of the oldest descriptions of the Christian Eucharist. It is brief but powerful. He asks an energetic question which calls for a great AMEN from all the church. "Is not the cup of blessing we bless a sharing in the blood of Christ? And is not the bread we break a sharing in the body of Christ? Because the loaf of bread is one, we, many though we are, are one body, for we all partake of the one loaf" (1 Corinthians 10:16–17).

Paul's summary of what Christians do around book and table suggests that there is a horizontal dimension to the Eucharist. In gathering, offering, blessing, breaking, pouring, eating, drinking, sharing, we are joined to the Christ who assembles us and whose Spirit lives both within the individual Christian and, importantly, in the gathered community. Thus we are joined one to another in the eucharistic activity. Because we are the body of Christ, we are united so intimately that loving service to one another is the is the logical consequence of what we have done and what we have become. At the eucharistic table, Christians are incorporated into Christ. Our lives are touched by and embodied into the very life of God.

In the celebration of the Eucharist, the statement that the community makes in gathering, blessing, and sharing is truly profound. We make a statement about who we are and what we hope to become. This hopeful statement sometimes highlights for us our own imperfection and the imperfection of both church and world. We come by our imperfection honestly. Though we are children of the light, we have first been touched by original darkness. So had the children of Israel who wandered in the darkness. Though God fed them with bread from heaven, they forgot about the slavery they had endured, and instead remembered fondly the fleshpots of Egypt. They told Moses how they missed "the fish we used to eat without cost in Egypt, and the cucumbers, the melons, the leeks, the onions, and the garlic" (Numbers 11:5). God reminded them that manna, that flat and dull food which nourished their bodies, also fed their freedom. The freedom of Christians in every age and place is fed by the life of Christ whom we are called to imitate. Jesus told us, "if you do not eat the flesh of the Son of Man and drink his blood, you have no life in you" (John 6:53).

Christians come to the eucharistic table wounded and sinful, but also hopeful and eager. Just as the manna in the desert strengthened the Israelites for their journey, so too does the eucharistic food and drink strengthen us. It is not just a collection of faces who come to the table, but a true assembly of gifted seekers. Each comes to this table with gifts and burdens. Each comes wounded, with memories both of gladness and of sorrow. But at the holy table we find one another and we find our true selves. We are given rest and nourishment. We struggle to make sense of the afflictions that burden and threaten to overwhelm us. There we encounter the hope and the promise that is a gift to all who participate.

Christians believe that we are the body of Christ. We who are fed at the eucharistic table believe that we will live forever. This insight provokes those seeking to develop a ministerial spirituality to continue feasting at the eucharistic table in all its mystery, majesty, memory, sustenance, and hope. At the table, we find not only the path to a developing and working spirituality, but we encounter our truest selves and the church in its highest and most noble manifestation.

Next, let us consider Lent and lenten preparations as a school for the development of a spirituality for ministry.

For Reflection and Discussion

- In your opinion, do most people see loving service as the logical consequence of celebrating the Eucharist? Why or why not?
- In what ways does the Eucharist strengthen you personally for your ministry?

PART FOUR

Feasts and Seasons

Smoke and Ashes

Direct our hearts to better things, O Lord;
heal our sin and ignorance.
Lord, do not face us suddenly with death,
but give us time to repent.
                ❦ Ash Wednesday responsory,
                          from the Sacramentary

Sometimes we make spirituality more work than is really necessary. This is the product, it seems to me, of the excessive individualism of our American culture. For example, I have a colleague who is exploring Christianity as he considers embracing it. He has, however, no guide, mentor, or spiritual director. He has discovered gnosticism (from the Greek *gnosis*, knowledge, or *gnostikos*, which means good at knowing), a heresy in which the knowledgeable saw themselves as a superior class of beings whose status was different from those who did not have their particular knowledge. The early church combated the many forms of gnosticism. Tertullian, in the second century, is usually regarded as the greatest foe of gnosticism in the early church. But my friend thinks there is much to recommend certain aspects of gnosticism and is currently exploring it. I admire his search and his tenacity and pray daily for him, but I tell him frankly that such a search for a spirituality that fits would exhaust me. I trust the church's conciliar judgments on gnosticism and all other heresies. I am content to live with a certain degree of trust and obedience.

I began to think of my friend's need to invent and discover one Sunday at Mass as I considered the seasons and the celebrations of the church year. In them we discover the keys and the tools to build a working spirituality. The cloud of smoke hanging in the air that Sunday morning was appalling. The South Bronx wasn't on fire, but the church seemed to be. The presider at the eucharistic table on this Sunday before Lent was enveloped in a cloud of dense smoke that seemed unwilling or unable to disseminate. It would not go away and invited recollections of Isaiah 4:5: "Then will the Lord create, over the whole site of Mount Zion and over her place of assembly, a smoking cloud by day and a light of flaming fire by night." I found the smoke and ash an invitation to consider our need to change and invent as we seek to grow spiritually.

The folks had undertaken a ceremonial making of ashes. The choir and ministers processed in and encircled the sanctuary space where a huge vat was filled with the palms that the throng of parishioners had brought from home. The presider had been asked to introduce what would unfold after the hymn and greeting. Then the parish director of religious education torched the palms. Those dry branches went up in a spectacular blaze in just a moment. The cantor led a rousing rendition of Psalm 51, and over the smoldering smudge pot, the priest prayed the blessing appointed for Ash Wednesday's ashes. All went to their places and continued with the opening prayer for the day.

All were ready to sing the final Gloria before Lent and to enter that holy season come Wednesday. Last year's palms were gone in a blaze; the ashes were waiting. The DRE was satisfied that the teachable had been taught while the church was at prayer: some sort of a new age *lex orandi, lex credendi* had been employed in service of a developing sensibility. Rituals grow up to meet perceived need. Sometimes the need may be that of a DRE who wants to connect life to liturgy, but does not recognize an immediate path. A ritual is then invented, a path blazed. Some such inventions work wonderfully. Some don't. Some of those that have worked and some that haven't become parish institutions, and after a few years seem to assume the force of law. The South Bronx and Harlem have the highest incidence of asthma in the nation. The atmosphere created in the church that day was certainly not helpful to anyone who suffered from any respiratory ailment. Had the church's interior paint not already been a dingy flaking gray, there would, no doubt, have been evidence on the walls of what was happening to our lungs.

Preparations for Ash Wednesday may be viewed as teachable moments for which there is no formal ritual. Most alert students believe that the Ash Wednesday's ashes are the residue of last year's palms. Most pastors know that the cup of ashes they burned and pushed through a sieve in the early years of Reagan's first term in the White House may well last several decades. What about an annual ritual burning of palms to provide fresh ash? Some say "No!" and point for support to the fact that there is no official ritual for the making of bread or of wine. On the other hand, the people of God who bake the eucharistic bread in their homes, convents, or rectories surely can and do pray and meditate over their holy tasks. The same is no doubt true for those who set the fermentation process in motion for the wine. This prayer would seem to be in the tradition of icon painters who fast and pray before and during their lovingly undertaken and prayerful labors.

A Symbolic Problem

The South Bronx fire was something of a symbolic problem. While the presider attempted to use it to point to the fire at Easter's Great Vigil, that pre-lenten blaze was really very different from the Vigil fire. It did not serve symbolically as purification from sinfulness or as the refiner's fire, nor did it stand as the symbol of light conquering darkness, or of Christ the light of the world. It only served functionally to reduce palm to ash. Where then is that bridge which one crosses in a pastoral fashion, honoring the members of the assembly, respecting the church's tradition, meeting the needs of the pious, providing for the education of children, and preserving peace and good will between pastors and other educators?

If those involved consider it important to prepare ashes with ritual activity, perhaps another model might be considered. In the Bronx, that same pot might have been kept burning on the porch of the church, attended to by high schoolers preparing for confirmation. Worshipers can be alerted to bring their palms and, as they enter the church on that Sunday just before Lent, can either toss their palms into the fire or hand them off to a student who will be glad to assist. Perhaps the ritual could be repeated for several weeks, or with certain classes or groups, to get people ready for the impending season.

There is for us, I think, a more important consideration than the creation of ashes in anticipation of Ash Wednesday: our need to invent. The ritual of the church is already really quite complete. That ritual needs proper implementation (the key!) more than it needs tinkering or new inventions. We have in our tradition and in our life of prayer both treasure and storehouse. Learning to trust that tradition and embrace that life of prayer is the stuff of true spirituality; conforming ourselves to Jesus as the church mediates his enduring, transforming presence is both spiritual path and goal, source and summit.

Next we will consider the power and joy of the lenten season as aspects of our ministerial role.

For Reflection and Discussion

- How does your parish celebrate Ash Wednesday? Are you able to help people relate the tradition of the church to their lives today?
- What "teachable moments" are most effective for you within the church's seasons?

Lent:
Power and Joy

Considering the path and message of the lenten season is another tool to guide us in forming a spirituality for ministry. We might begin by asking: Could it be the apple's fault? Did the apple provoke the woman into sin? Is the apple the culprit? Doesn't sound reasonable. The apple can't think. An apple has no power over me. Didn't over her, either. Is the devil at fault? "The devil made me do it" is a popular excuse. But it is no more than an excuse. Evil might be suggestive and even enticing, but it can't make me do anything I don't want to do. Can't make you do it, either.

How about Eve? Is it the fault of a woman that sin entered the world? Even the freed slave turned abolitionist and emancipationist, Sojourner Truth, seemed to suggest that women were the cause of sin's entry into the world: "If one woman could turn creation on its ear in the beginning," she wondered, "imagine what all women working together could accomplish." Some readers find an anti-woman bias in Genesis, but it could hardly be the divine intention to suggest that women are the reason that sin has come to earth. We understand that human invitation, free will exercised by men and women, our poor and irresponsible human choices, have caused the long reign of sin. Not the apple. Not the evil one. Not the woman. We do what our ancestors have done: we make selfish choices, and we impede the coming of the fullness of the reign of God.

Genesis tells us the problem and invites us to reflect on the sad presence of sin in the human community and its effects on our lives today and in every generation. Jesus tells us what to do about sin, how society's current order must be turned on its head, fortunes reversed, power used in new ways, tyrants overthrown, and tyranny forsaken. Jesus, of course, is both model and inspiration. His fast in the desert calls our attention to how power is best used. We might be puzzled by the fast of Jesus in the desert over those forty days. Jesus "fasted forty days and forty nights, and afterwards he was famished. The tempter came and said to him, 'If you are the Son of God, command these stones to become loaves of bread'" (Matthew 4:2). Why, we might wonder, was it such a bad idea to turn those stones to bread? So, what's the big deal? Is the idea a bad one because it comes from a bad source? Many puzzle over this one on the first Sunday of Lent when this reading is traditionally proclaimed. Really, John's gospel assures us that the Word of God was present at creation when the Spirit hovered over the deep. So, the Word, Jesus, with the Father and in the Spirit, is responsible for all of creation. How big a deal would it be to turn a few stones into some delicious bread?

That simple task was not a possibility in the Lord's plan. In the desert, confronted by the tempter, Jesus would not call angels to deliver bread when he fasted. This was not how the Messiah's reign was to begin. If Jesus had, in fact, turned stones into bread, he would have been using his power for his own benefit. Jesus did not do that. Not then. Not ever. He did not save himself from the cross. His power was used on behalf of God's people. His power was never used selfishly, but only for others. There is our model for the appropriate use of power.

Jesus and Power

So a keen understanding of power was part of the plan of Jesus in creating a new order in society. Power would always be used for "us," never just for me. Power unites us and quickens us to do all things in justice. Any use of power that does not seek to serve justice and advance God's reign is an abuse of power. Here is a case in point. Remember the reaction of thoughtful New Yorkers after the tragic death of Amadou Diallo in 1999? It seems apparent that he died unjustly at the hands of officers who were not serving, protecting, or defending. Their use of power seems not to have followed the motto seen on the side of the police cruisers, "CPR: courtesy, professionalism, respect." Commenting sadly, the late Cardinal John O'Connor said, "We have gone mad with violence."

We experience the world as it is, and not as the world should be. Many of our church groups call us to an appropriate use of our own power. Not in retaliation. Not seeking vengeance. In imitation of Jesus, we are called to exercise the power that is ours, power that comes from God and that no one else can give. This power enables us to see the world as it is and transform it, working with God's good Spirit, into the world as it ought to be. Power properly exercised calls us into interaction with others, not dominance over others. We are called to build relationships. The family and the church are examples of power in relationship: we protect the weakest, favor the poorest, engage our power to overthrown tyranny, and introduce a new way of living among all God's people.

We ponder then the answer of Jesus to the devil in the desert: "It is written, one does not live by bread alone, but by every word that comes from the mouth of God" (Matthew 4:4). The word of God directs us to work for a common purpose, not to fight among ourselves or to answer violence with violence. Our task, as God's love in the world, is to use power to bring justice. With Jesus as our model, we understand that power is not for us alone, but to be exercised on behalf of the community.

Jesus teaches that "the reign of God is already in your midst" (Luke 17:21). Who then can enter the kingdom of God? It is those who experience *metanoia*, a change of mind, of heart, of attitude. The days of Lent call us to that change that we might come refreshed and renewed to the Easter feast with a better grip on what it means to seek, develop, and live a spirituality that will feed our ministerial lives. We will find great power in the words of Jesus. If all those who consider themselves his followers were to live in conformity to his words for a full day, the world as we know it would be launched into a new orbit. The faith of Jesus and the possibility of God's reign continue to quicken our hope in the developing earth, in the promise of peace, in the transformation of culture.

An Explosive Message

Jesus knew that his message was explosive, and that those who would hear and follow would not be silent. In fact, he was told during his entry into Jerusalem that he should rebuke his disciples. Apparently they were too loud and embarrassing for the sedate and orderly city residents. The entire crowd of disciples was shouting "Blessed is he who comes / in the name of the Lord! / Peace in heaven and glory in the highest heaven" (Luke 19:38–39). The complainers did not associate this cry with the very similar message of the angels to the shepherds earlier in Luke after the birth of the infant (2:14). Jesus, of course, made the connection, and he told the Pharisees who would have the disciples be still that "If they were to keep silence, I tell you the very stones would cry out" (19:40). Their cry would be in joy at the presence of the one in whom all the earth will find salvation.

And this one, Jesus, calls us to be people of power. The power that will transform the face of the earth is not in the apple, or in the evil one, but in me and in you and in all who seek a new understanding of spirituality for service. We ask God on the First Sunday of Lent to bring us back to the life Jesus won for us. Here is God's power, God's gift to us, that will bring light and peace and joy to all the world. These considerations, it seems to me, explain the church's reasons for seeing Lent as a time of joy. The first lenten preface to the eucharistic prayer reminds us that each year God gives us this joyful season so we can prepare to celebrate the paschal mystery with minds and hearts renewed. Walking this liturgical path with eyes wide open will guide and form us as we come to know the Way who is Jesus.

Next we consider whether or not to build a "bigger barn" as we wait for Christ in joyful hope.

For Reflection and Discussion

- How do you experience the power of Lent? Is it more a time of repentance or of joy? Why?
- What does *metanoia* mean to you personally? How does it apply to your ministry?

A Time for Resurrection

Then [the rich man] said, "I will do this: I will pull down my barns and build larger ones, and there I will store all my grain and my goods. And I will say to my soul, 'Soul, you have ample goods laid up for many years; relax, eat, drink, be merry.'" But God said to him, "You fool! This very night your life is being demanded of you. And the things you have prepared, whose will they be?" So it is with those who store up treasures for themselves but are not rich in the eyes of God.

❧ Luke 12:18–21

St. Benedict, the father of western monasticism, advises the monks in his "Rule for Monasteries" to keep death ever before their eyes. This insight sent me to an estate sale recently and I found the outing a good time to reflect on the brevity of life and the courage required to embrace the truth of Easter. I've been to only a few estate sales, and now I've figured out why. It's alarming to realize that the mementos of a lifetime are spread out for strangers to view—strangers who most often did not know or care about the one who has died, strangers who are looking for a bargain and for whom these mementos hold no memories.

Actually we weren't all strangers at this particular sale. There were several old and frail ladies who were obviously not in the market for any keepsakes, but who knew the dead owner. These elders took great delight in poking around parts of the house where they had never been, observing that "Ethel used wheat germ, too, but she bought the great big jars." There was a bottle of Pepto-Bismol for sale. Like the wheat germ, it was the large economy size. I wondered why someone old and frail would buy the large size. It seemed to me that the odds were not in favor of the owner living long enough to take all the medicine in that very large bottle. Did she not know that death was coming? Was she not prepared to greet it? Did she think that buying the large size would ward off death until she had soothed minor ailments with the pink liquid?

This estate sale was part of my meditation throughout Lent, and I brought it to the weeks of Easter. Easter is the promise that death will visit each of us. More, it is the assurance that death does not complete life, but changes it. Easter prompts us to recall, from the darkest of grief to life's smallest trials, how God comforts us and gives us the courage to persevere. Our Easter faith encourages us to ask the proper questions and to leave unasked those which have no answers. If we ask, "How can God allow suffering and tragedy?" or "why is there evil in the world?" we will find no answers. Pursuing such questions, we may only find bitterness and anger: the questions will remain unanswered.

Faith Is Our Guide

Faith reminds us, in all disappointments and especially in grief, to thank God for love, affection, compassion and all good gifts. Faith demands that we remember the goodness enjoyed in years that are sometimes too short and too few, but can also be too long and pain-filled. Faith instructs us to accept our lives as the most precious gift of all. The promise of Easter is the promise of resurrection, that from death will come new life. Easter faith prompts us to recall yesterday with gratitude, look toward tomorrow with courage and hope, and celebrate daily the moments God has given us.

I recalled that outing and meditation on a recent August Saturday when I went for a morning swim before heading off to the parish to share weekend duties. Before jumping in, I stood in the northern Minnesota lake in cool water up to my waist. There were no clouds in the sky, no boats or personal watercrafts on the lake, not another swimmer in sight, nor anyone visible on shore. A certain peace enfolded me, and the concerns and anxieties of the day slipped away. I put aside the not-quite-complete homily, the urgency of grocery shopping for dinner, the prospect of the impending return to the classroom: all of these faded away in the presence of grace.

In a flash, and without thinking about it, I understood the mystical Julian of Norwich's comforting promise: "all shall be well, and all shall be well, and all manner of things shall be well." I felt a deep and abiding sense of gratitude and a call to offer thanksgiving, and knew that I was rich in the things that matter to God. And just then I resolved to delay indefinitely all plans to build a bigger barn.

Next we will consider what we learn and how our spiritual path is formed while celebrating the Triduum.

For Reflection and Discussion

- How do you respond to the words of Julian of Norwich: "All shall be well, and all shall be well, and all manner of things shall be well"?
- How can these words be reconciled with the sureness of death? How do you share this message in your ministry?

The Paschal Mystery

I listened to an Easter sermon once in which a preacher stood up in front of a church full of people hungry for good news and told us Easter bunny jokes, one after another. He never met our eyes. He looked up at the light fixtures as he delivered his punch lines, never noticing how we laughed less and less each time. Finally he said something about how Easter was God's joke on death and we should all laugh more. Then he said Amen and sat down. I have never in my life wished so badly for pulpit police. I wanted someone with a badge to go up and arrest that guy, slap some handcuffs on him, and lead him away.

≈ Barbara Brown Taylor

I recently dipped a newborn into the baptismal waters. The experience provoked in me, as it should, a reconsideration of life in the church both as a member and as a pastoral minister. I then took another look at the Triduum which invites us year by year both to celebrate the joy that is ours in belonging to Christ and to one another, and to meditate on what such belonging means. Back for a moment to the baby: she was lifted up out of the baptismal water, dried off, anointed with chrism announcing her royal status, and dressed in the finery befitting her status as a daughter of God. Then, for some reason, her godfather leaned over to me and whispered conspiratorially, "I used to be an altar boy, Father, so let me know if you need any help." I smiled, thanked him, handed him the baptismal candle and pointed to the paschal candle; he knew immediately to light hers from the Light of Christ. He thought, perhaps, that he had helped. He had only just begun. The ritual admonition that followed outlined the help that he was called to give. But it was not an altar boy's assistance, nor was it help to the baptizing priest.

After the candle has been lighted, the minister tells the parents and godparents that this light is entrusted to them to be kept burning brightly and that this child of theirs has been enlightened by Christ. She is to walk always as a child of the light and with their help keep the flame of faith alive in her heart. He prays too that when the Lord comes, the child may go out to meet him with all the saints in heaven.

These parents and godparents, having answered affirmatively when asked, "Is it your will that this child should be baptized in the faith of the church, which we have all professed with you?" were undertaking to bring her up in the practice of the faith, seeing that the divine life that God gives her is kept safe from sin and nurtured so that it will continue to grow.

God's grace and the church's assistance are offered to the parents and godparents in their awesome responsibilities in the final blessing. The minister prays that God may continue to pour out blessings upon these sons and daughters of his and make them faithful members of the church.

What we were about in this ritual moment is well explained by the rite itself. We use the Latin *lex orandi, lex credendi* to suggest that the church's prayer both explicates and shapes what the church believes. Each baptism points to the Easter feast, and each year as Easter approaches, we might profitably look to the rites of the Triduum to explain what we believe about the passion, death, and Resurrection of Jesus, and our own place in that Paschal Mystery. This should be an annual exercise, I believe, for all of us in pastoral ministry.

Our Place in the Mystery

Vatican II solemnly declared what the folks who take Genesis and the Sabbath rest seriously already knew to be true, that the proper use of just about anything can work toward our salvation. Thus, for well-disposed members of the faithful, the liturgy of the sacraments and sacramentals sanctifies almost every event in their lives. They are given access to the stream of divine grace which flows from the paschal mystery of the passion, death, and Resurrection of Christ, the font from which all sacraments and sacramentals draw their power. There is hardly any proper use of material things that cannot thus be directed toward the sanctification of all people and the praise of God.

This is a teaching to enrich and enliven both peaks and valleys, the days and the decades of our lives. I was prompted to remember it by a summer note. A friend wrote to say, "I avoid mirrors as I round the curve toward sixty. I was recently at a surprise birthday gathering in Minneapolis for a high school classmate, and I wondered, who are all these old fat bald guys? Age is taking its toll on me in many ways. That may be part of the Triduum story: 'Death is stalking us all.' Jesus, against Satchel Paige's advice, turned and faced death, captured the energy of fear it wields over us and grappled the whole thing to a standstill, not unlike Jacob. We are all going to die, but we can seize the meaning of death, rename it love, offer it for the sake of the community, come away wounded but with a new destiny. Something like that."

This man sends me to the Triduum with mind and heart renewed.

Mass of the Lord's Supper

> *We should glory in the cross of our Lord Jesus Christ,*
> *for he is our salvation, our life and our resurrection;*
> *through him we are saved and made free.*
>   ❧ INTRODUCTORY RITES (SEE GALATIANS 6:14)

The rubrics for Holy Thursday remind us that the tabernacle should be entirely empty; a sufficient amount of bread should be consecrated at the Mass for the communion of clergy and laity on this day and

Good Friday. As we come to this day mindful of our Jewish roots, might this instruction not remind us of the directions for the Passover which call for the home to be swept clean so that all leavened products are removed? We begin our eucharistic action this night knowing that we begin again, remembering and celebrating the new Passover of cross and Resurrection, the ultimate word of truth and love: ancient mystery, ever new.

We are also instructed that during the singing of the Gloria, the church bells are rung but then will remain silent until the Easter Vigil. Catholics of a certain age often wondered (and heard various answers) about when Lent actually ended. This rubric settles it. Lent ends as we begin the Triduum. We still fast on Good Friday and until the Vigil begins, but it is not the lenten fast of penance and preparation, but an anticipatory fast. The *Constitution on the Sacred Liturgy* alerts us to the distinction when it explains that during Lent penance should not be only internal and individual, but also external and social. The practice of penance should be fostered in ways that are possible in our own times and in different regions, and according to the circumstances of the faithful (Article 22).

It also emphasizes that the paschal fast should be kept sacred and celebrated everywhere on Good Friday and, where possible, prolonged throughout Holy Saturday. Why? So that the joys of Easter Sunday resurrection can be attained with uplifted and clear minds.

The next rubric is very specific: "The washing of the feet follows the homily." For reasons that seem to contradict the gospel, some presiders invite people to wash their hands instead. Jesus has already ruled on this practice in his reply to Peter in John's gospel proclaimed just moments before: "Simon Peter said to him, 'Lord, not my feet only but also my hands and my head!' Jesus said to him, 'He who has bathed does not need to wash, except for his feet…'" (13:9–10).

Some congregations omit this ritual foot washing entirely. It is hard to give a reason to support their innovation given the response of Jesus to Peter who had first wanted no part of the ritual: "Peter said to him, 'You shall never wash my feet.' Jesus answered him, 'If I do not wash you, you have no part in me'" (John 13:8).

Note also the directive: "At the beginning of the liturgy of the Eucharist, there may be a procession of the faithful with gifts for the poor." Could there be a day better suited for such a procession with checks and cash, foodstuffs, clothing, and whatever else might be needed locally, nationally, or internationally?

Note, too, that the Mass concludes with the prayer after communion. The transfer of the Holy Eucharist follows. After a period of silent adoration, the priest and ministers genuflect and return to the sacristy. There is neither blessing nor dismissal on this day. We are going home, but this liturgy is spread over three days; there will be no dismissal until the conclusion of the Vigil.

Celebration of the Lord's Passion

> *Lord,*
> *by shedding his blood for us,*
> *your Son, Jesus Christ,*
> *established the paschal mystery.*
> *In your goodness, make us holy*
> *and watch over us always.*
> *We ask this through Christ our Lord.*
>
> ✥ Prayer, Passion Celebration

This celebration begins without procession or greeting and with the prayer given above. On this day particularly, note that in the General Intercessions, we pray for the Jewish people, the first to hear the word of God. Our prayer is that they may continue to grow in love of God's name and in faithfulness to God's covenant. We also ask God to listen to the church as we pray that the Jewish people may arrive at the fullness of redemption. This prayer alerts us to the reverence we owe to our ancestors in the faith and assures us that the gift of salvation in Christ can and will be mediated as God alone chooses. John Paul II, in *Crossing the Threshold of Hope*, reminds us of this truth when he writes that God acts in the sacraments as well as in other ways known to God alone (#134).

As the cross is venerated, we might remember the command given to Moses as he approached the burning bush: "Do not come near; put off your shoes from your feet, for the place on which you are standing is holy ground" (Exodus 3:5). When I was a child, our pastor would always take off his shoes and instruct the servers to do the same as they approached the cross. Perhaps this is a practice to imitate at least in Spirit.

As a pastor myself, I invited confirmation candidates—these would be high school students in my home diocese—to carry the cross into the church and accompany it with lighted candles as the rubrics suggest. We would add bowls of incense as well, but these would be carried only by young women whose presence would call to mind the myrrh-bearing women who went to the tomb that first Easter morning, the women who had remained faithfully at the foot of the cross when the male disciples deserted. I was always pleased to have these students hold the cross, candles, and incense as the congregation came forward. I wanted them to witness and be in awe of the expressed faith of the faithful as they knelt, genuflected, bowed before, touched, or kissed the wood of the cross. As a faithful people, we have few moments when we more reverently express ourselves in gratitude to the one who saves and sets us free.

There are some who suggest that the "Reproaches" (poignant poem-like chants of very ancient origin) should be omitted; they view these antiphons and responses as anti-Semitic. They are incorrect. The Reproaches are no more anti-Semitic than the Passover Seder is anti-Egyptian. In fact, the Reproaches should be compared, I think, to the hymn *Dayaynu* sung at the Passover. In this litany, the leader enumerates the blessings God has given the chosen people, beginning with the Sabbath rest and deliverance from Egypt. The participants respond to each remembered blessing by singing Dayaynu, "we would have been content," or, "it would have been enough." The Reproaches borrow this model. Jesus speaks from the cross, "My people, what have I done to you? / How have I offended you? Answer me!" He enumerates the blessings God has given in every age, beginning with the deliverance from Egypt, and adds, "but you led your Savior to the cross," and the refrain is repeated. The last of the Reproaches is "I raised you to the height of majesty, but you have raised me high on a cross." And the refrain is sung once more: "My people, what have I done to you?"

After communion, all depart in silence. For the remainder of the day and on Holy Saturday, the church waits at the Lord's tomb, reflecting on his suffering and death.

The Great Vigil

Dear friends in Christ,
on this most holy night,
when our Lord Jesus Christ passed from death to life,
the church invites her children throughout the world
to come together in vigil and prayer.
This is the Passover of the Lord:
if we honor the memory of his death and resurrection
by hearing his word and celebrating his mysteries,
then we may be confident
that we shall share his victory over death
and live with him forever in God.
   ⚘ SOLEMN BEGINNING OF THE VIGIL

The Vigil is celebrated during the night, held in anticipation of the Resurrection, and it is only after the solemn vigil that the Easter celebration begins, with a spirit of joy that continues for a period of fifty days. Attending this great Vigil is inconvenient, as is much of religious life, and may not be possible for the elderly or infirm for whom evening activities are difficult or even impossible. Yet, it is the conclusion of the liturgy begun on Thursday evening (though the Triduum itself ends after evening prayer on Sunday), and it is an extraordinary time to invite Catholics into fuller, deeper participation in the life of the church.

The fire that is blessed as the Vigil begins recalls Luke's gospel story (12:35ff), which reminds us to have our lamps burning ready as we await the bridegroom. The rubric advises that this large fire burn in a suitable place outside the church. Why not have the fire burning as the folks assemble, perhaps kindled earlier by Boy or Girl Scouts who are eager to earn badges as they serve the church?

As the baptismal water is blessed, there is an electrifying moment when the priest or deacon lowers the Easter candle into the water as the priest prays, "We ask you, Father with your Son / to send the Holy Spirit upon the waters of this font." The baptismal font, the womb of the church, receives her Christ, and we emerge from the water as the first fruits of their union. This fecundity is remembered in the special form of the first eucharistic prayer's *hanc igitur* for the Easter Octave, reminding us that those born of this union of Christ and the church rise from the baptismal water "born into the new life of water and the Holy Spirit with all their sins forgiven." In this context, the enthusiasm in 1 Peter seems acutely understated: "There is cause for rejoicing here" (1:6).

Celebrating the Resurrection

I have risen: I am with you once more;
you placed your hand on me to keep me safe.
How great is the depth of your wisdom, alleluia!
                    ◈ Easter Sunday, Introductory Rites
                              (Psalm 138:18, 5–6)

When I was teaching at Lewis University in suburban Chicago, I was inspired by an insightful theology major who reflected in class and later in an e-mail exchange on the relationship of Passover to Eucharist, considering the implications of what is celebrated in the Triduum. He pointed to George Bernanos's novel, *The Diary of a Country Priest*. In it, the priest wisely observes, "Grace is everywhere." "We, too," wrote young Nick Macak, "in all of these celebrations, interact with the grace of God present all around us." Receptivity to and interaction with grace are concepts and opportunities that ought to give us pause, or Sabbath rest. His realization prompts the opening prayer on Easter Sunday morning: "Let our celebration today / raise us up and renew our lives / by the Spirit that is within us."

What does this renewed life look like? The Spanish prayer after communion for the twenty-seventh Sunday in Ordinary Time puts it succinctly in a way that quickens our hope: *Que esta comunión, Señor, / sacie nuestra hambre y nuestra sed de ti, / y nos transforme en tu Hijo, Jesúscristo, / que vive y reina por los siglos de los siglos.* My translation: "May this communion, Lord, / satisfy our hunger and our thirst for you, / and transform us into your Son, Jesus Christ, / who lives and reigns forever and ever." The English Sacramentary has us pray instead: "Almighty God, / let the Eucharist we share / fill us with your life. / May the love of Christ which we celebrate here / touch our lives and lead us to you."

The original prayer in Latin is: *Concede nobis, omnipotens Deus, / ut de perceptis sacramentis inebriemur atque pascamur, / quaetenus in id quod sumimus transeamus.* In private correspondence, Lauren Pristas, PhD, of New Jersey's Caldwell College, notes that *inebriare* is the root of our word inebriate—it can mean to make drunk, but can also mean to water or to saturate or drench with any liquid. She translates the prayer: "Grant us, almighty God, / that we may be saturated and nourished by the sacraments we have received, / so that we may be transformed into that which we have consumed."

We are what we eat. The church, radiant, risen from the water, says, "Amen!" And in this paschal journey and feast, we see both trajectory (from here to eternity) and cycle (Advent to *eschaton* or last days), and therein we find our spiritual path.

Next we will consider solicitude and prudence in maintaining and passing on our traditions.

For Reflection and Discussion

- Which day of the Triduum is most meaningful to you personally? Why is this?
- In what ways are you "saturated and nourished" by the sacraments you receive? Do you think people in general experience sacraments this way?

PART FIVE

Seeking a Spirituality

Unity and Charity

*If you continue in my word,
   you are truly my disciples;
and you will know the truth,
   and the truth will make you free.*

※ JOHN 8:31–32

People both to the right and to the left of us are often afflicted with a "certainty" that can be noxious and toxic. If we are not careful in our own dealings, watchful of our own tongues, faithful to our own prayer and compassion, even when neither is pleasurable, we will not develop a healthy spirituality, one that will support and guide us not just in the pleasures of ministry, but in the grind of duty on days that seem dark. The recollected wisdom of Tammany Hall was that morning glories and reformers both wilt by noon. But we who seek to follow and live in Jesus will not wilt at noon even when our resolve is tested by those who in their "certainty" often seem uncharitable or unjust. Living with them in charity is the fruit of a well-formed and well-lived spirituality.

Recently in a parish where I was visiting, an administrator showed me the parish newsletter, which featured a "Why Do Catholics Do That?" column. One question was about why the priest or deacon adds water to the wine during the preparation of the gifts. The answer was correctly and intelligibly delivered, though the newsletter did not quote the prayer prayed while the water is poured (thus violating

"Graham's Dictum for Explaining Church Stuff": Always begin with the prayer attached to the act!). In this instance, the prayer is the perfect explanation of why the water is added: "By the mystery of this water and wine, may we come to share in the divinity of Christ who humbled himself to share in our humanity." A very certain and pious, if not erudite, member of the parish came to the office with her copy of the newsletter corrected by her in red ink with the notation, "This is not the truth!!!" She quoted Sister Faustina as her source, but the reference she used was unrelated to the question at hand. There was no humility in her approach, and even though she was a high school graduate many years earlier with no theological or liturgical education, she asserted that her piety was the true teacher. She was wrong, unjust, and uncharitable, and she left a crowd of workers steaming in her wake.

Cultivating Prudence

Such instances are common in parish life. Thus newly appointed pastors and pastoral workers soon learn that in addition to pastoral solicitude, they need also to cultivate a certain prudence (though they may hesitate to quote Matthew 10:16: "See, I am sending you out like sheep into the midst of wolves; so be wise as serpents and innocent as doves"), as well as an appreciation for the issues involved in maintaining and passing on our traditions and in building and fortifying a spirituality to assist us in that task.

Posture during the eucharistic prayer is often another source of conflict. Some are outraged by what they see as liberal deviance in standing as the prayer is offered. But cloistered nuns who lie prostrate during the same prayer, broadcasting the liturgy by satellite from their cloister on their own television network, are not similarly criticized. Who are the dangerous liberals here really? If one examines the ancient eucharistic prayer of Hippolytus, one discovers that we who offer it count ourselves blessed "to stand in your presence and serve you." The prayer of Hippolytus, reworked just a bit, is the second eucharistic prayer in the Sacramentary of Paul VI issued after Vatican II. The prayer was written about AD 231 and certainly seems to suggest that standing was the approved posture in the third century in Rome. Examination of St. Peter's Basilica in Vatican City, and watching televised papal Masses elsewhere, suggest that the posture is also currently acceptable in other places. While the bishops of the United States want congregants to kneel during the prayer, and while this posture is also certainly acceptable as is the call to obedience, one must admit that standing, while contrary to local law, is neither an abomination nor an innovation. Lying prostrate, however, seems to have no precedent.

And don't even get me started on television cameras in cloisters. What's that all about anyway? Why invite a television camera into a cloister, much less run a television network from one, sitting for chats with the viewing public? Who gave permission for such an innovation? How are the vocations of cloistered contemplative, network executive, and talk-show host compatible?

And obedience to lawful authority? Imagine if a member or leader of "Call to Action" boldly asserted in a public forum with a national audience that the cardinal archbishop of Los Angeles deserves "zero obedience"! How is it then that such a charge can actually be made on cable television by a nun who remains unrepentant? People tend to overlook this because the accuser is "conservative." But what is she conserving? Rarely has the American church seen such an outrage. Comments like hers are a threat to unity and good order, not to mention charity.

Other Cases in Point

A young seminarian, still at work on his bachelor's degree, once accused his theology professor of some heresy or other. Asked how it was possible that someone who had only six credits of theology under his biretta (and all six credits from the accused's classroom!) could discern the deficiencies of someone with three advanced degrees in theology, including a doctorate, and who also had the grace of holy orders to which the seminarian aspired, he could not explain. How it was possible that he knew so much more, he could not say, but he declared that he did know! The consequent disarray was the opposite of unity.

Another seminarian reports that he and his cohort could not attend the Eucharist at their seminary when a certain priest presided because they had judged that the priest could not validly celebrate the Eucharist. Asked what particular offense this man had committed, they replied that he omitted at daily Mass the embolism which follows the Lord's prayer: "Deliver us, Oh Lord, from every evil." In their judgment, this omission rendered the Eucharist invalid. They were shown the ritual for marriage, and it was pointed out that in the nuptial Mass, the rubrics indicate that the embolism is to be omitted and that the Lord's Prayer is to be followed by the wedding blessing. Obviously then omitting the embolism does not invalidate the Eucharist. Unless, that is, these seminarians believe, like the followers of the wildly liberal but excommunicated, late Archbishop Marcel Lefebvre, that the Second Vatican Council was "hijacked by Modernists." Otherwise, they seem to have unjustly accused a priest of heresy when he is not even guilty of *errans in fide* (an error in the faith). Never mind the disrespect they show to the archbishop who sent the priest to the seminary as a staff member. If he were involved with heretical practices, the archbishop would be complicit. As it stands, the seminarian seemed to be questioning the archbishop's good sense as well as his orthodoxy.

But imagine Archbishop Lefebvre's dilemma. He believed that outside the church there is no salvation. But he placed himself outside the church by ordaining bishops for his movement without direction or permission from the Holy See. One hopes that God's quality of mercy and tenderness goes beyond the image of it that the archbishop himself reflected. But the scandal of division? And how is it that someone can be regarded as conservative who asserts that the Spirit speaks more distinctly to him than to all the rest of the world's bishops and the pope, even when they gather in sacred council? The man and his movement, and those who ape his fear and anger while remaining within the Roman church, think, possibly, that because "we proclaim Christ crucified, a stumbling block to Jews and foolishness to Gentiles" (1 Corinthians 1:23) that there may be some virtue in being a stumbling block. But in their outrage, they seem to forget the promise of Christ to Peter, that "on this rock I will build my church, and the gates of Hades will not prevail against it" (Matthew 16:18). To forget or rework the words of Jesus? To suggest that one knows better than the Messiah or the Spirit? The worst kind of liberalism. Talk about cafeteria Catholicism!

The Common Ground

In these examples, where is the common ground that the late Cardinal Joseph Bernadin encouraged us to seek? While previous generations made disputes with those they termed "the separated brethren," today greeted with dignity and respect, now we Catholics seem to engage one another in a certain warfare that is not helpful to the church or any individual member. Those who see themselves as conservative seem to suggest that no conversation is necessary since they have both pope and truth in their corner. Others, characterized as liberals, are often ready for dialogue, thinking that when members of the opposing camp listens long enough, they will at last be converted. Together both camps need to seek the truth that liberates. Remember that Jesus said to those who believed in him, "If you continue in my word, you are truly my disciples; and you will know the truth, and the truth will make you free" (John 8:31–32).

It seems to me that one needs a healthy dose of charity plus a modicum of humor to survive church life, for the infallibility with which so many of us seem to vest ourselves is evidence not of our wisdom and piety, but of our pride. Learning to listen respectfully, to dialogue carefully, to be shaped by what we pray are the fruits of the spirituality we seek to cultivate.

Next we will consider what happens when Christianity is worn as a burden rather than experienced as joy.

For Reflection and Discussion

- Have you had encounters with people who have either misconstrued or misunderstood your message? What did you do?
- How do you achieve "unity" with those you serve? What might you do to improve a sense of unity?

Standing for Human Dignity

God our Father,
You will all [people] to be saved,
and come to the knowledge of your truth.
Send workers into your great harvest
that the gospel may be preached to every creature
and your people,
> *gathered together by the word of life*
and strengthened by the power of the sacraments,
may advance in the way of salvation and love.
> ✥ Opening prayer,
> Mass for the Spread of the Gospel

There are in our church many needs and many issues, and all of them call for an awareness and understanding of human dignity. When we ignore human dignity, serious problems begin. Attentiveness to human dignity is the beginning of every solution. I thought of this truth as I pondered the problem of the priest who visited one of his favorite congregations in northern Minnesota over Christmas. He enjoys celebrating the Eucharist with and preaching to this lively group and appreciates the animated and friendly discussions that follow each celebration. Preaching on the feast of the Holy Family, he relied on Walter J. Burghardt's "Christmas Message" (*America*, Dec. 20, 1997) in which he quotes Pope John Paul II: "In the Christian view, our treatment of children becomes a measure of our fidelity to the Lord himself, the Lord who asserted 'Whoever welcomes one such child in my name welcomes me'" (Matthew 18:5).

Burghardt asserts that in the United States, the richest country on earth, the most vulnerable among us are our children. On that frosty Minnesota morning, it was alarming to hear that some sixteen million children (almost four times the population of the state) live below the poverty line, and perhaps a million had slept the night before on America's streets. Burghardt adds, and the preacher repeated, that a million and a half unborn are forcibly prevented each year from ever gracing a crib. Repeating this staggering statistic, he glanced at a local abortion opponent seated firmly on his right a third of the way back in the nave. He had never seen her smile and she seemed to wear her Christianity more as a burden than as a joy. But he thought that this morning he was singing from her hymnal and she would have to acknowledge a Holy Family homily well preached.

She left the church without a word to him.

On New Year's Day, she was back in her accustomed spot and looked prepared to listen critically as he approached the pulpit. Getting great mileage out of his *America* subscription and one December issue, he relied on Dennis Hamm's "The Word" column, in which he asks "Who Is a Child of God?" Hamm makes reference to Stanley Hauerwas's modest proposal that Christians resolve not to kill other Christians. Such an attitude, writes Hamm, would have made a great impact on recent history. He points to Rwanda, and the preacher made reference to a seminary classmate, now a Navy chaplain, who had presided at a funeral liturgy and helped dig the graves for a bishop and large number of priests martyred in that particular conflict. The preacher repeated Hamm's assertion that if we Christians would recognize each other as adopted children of God, we might more easily recognize the image of God in the rest of humankind. Not a risky assertion, he thought, and certainly to the point on a day when we pray for world peace.

The anti-abortion lady did approach him on that particular holy day, the first time she had ever approached him after hearing (or, perhaps, enduring) him on any number of Sundays. She came close as he was greeting congregants moving out of the church and offered a hand.

"Father, don't you agree," she asked, firmly clasping his hand in both of hers, watching his face closely, "that abortion is the worst kind of killing?"

"Well," he mumbled, caught off guard and very much surprised, "it certainly is very bad."

A Stunned Response

He walked away stunned. She had heard him firmly assert on the previous Sunday, quoting Pope John Paul II (who, Burghardt asserts and the preacher repeated, puts the problem bluntly), that our treatment of children, including those unborn, becomes a measure of our fidelity to the Lord himself. Even while we decry abortion, may we not also say that for Catholics to kill Catholics in Rwanda and for Catholics and Protestants to make war in Ireland is bad as well?

At first, he reports that he was angry because of the zealot's focus on a single issue. But his anger grew in scope. "How dare you," he asked as he made mental lists of what he could and might or should have said. "How dare you ask a priest, vested, moments from the altar, if his view is consistent with what the church, and he with her, clearly teaches?" "How dare you fail to mention the previous homily, for which you were present, which answered the question you now ask so disingenuously?" "How dare you administer, semipublicly, a litmus test for compatibility with your own narrowly defined vision of orthodoxy?" "How dare you compromise the church's attention to this significant issue by declaring a battleground in which everyone who is not an anti-abortion terrorist is branded as a pro-abortion murderer?" "How dare you?"

We are a church that includes some zany members as well as folks who are sometimes hurtful in their pursuit of the gospel call as they hear it. And we might accept as a personal problem that we let them get to us so. If it is a contest, they win. Many pastoral workers report they find such critics among the most wearying features of pastoral service, the poor we always have with us. We can be amazed at politicians and bishops and pastors who really seem to let what sounds like mean-spirited criticism roll off their backs. But some folks can't.

In his reflection for the Feast of the Holy Family that same year, Hamm reminds us that being family is an intimate involvement with the divine. This involvement, he concludes, is more challenging than we expect, more promising than we could hope for. "And always we need outside help."

A recent *New York Times*/CBS poll suggests that twenty-five years and nearly thirty million abortions after Roe v. Wade, forty-five percent of the American public believes that abortion is more of an issue involving the life of the fetus, while forty-four percent believe that abortion is more an issue involving a woman's ability to control her body. What good can come of the forty-five percent bickering and casting accusations and aspersions among ourselves? If there is to be world peace, if we are to be God's family, relying on divine assistance, there'll first need to be some healing between the fellow in the presider's chair and the woman seated at his right a third of the way back in the nave. Who would have thought that human dignity could be at issue in the exchange between preacher and congregant? We should observe ourselves in our interactions with those we find difficult. As we examine our motives and our consciences day by day, we will see that living with those we have not chosen, or would not choose, in peace and with charity is the fruit of a well-formed and well-lived spirituality.

Next we will consider being careful about what we do or say in our ministry—and where we do or say it.

For Reflection and Discussion

- What is your reaction to "one issue" parishioners?
- What do you think of the priest's reaction? Why do you think it bothered him so much?

"Manner" and Manners

> *Let no evil talk come out of your mouths, but only what is useful for building up, as there is need, so that your words may give grace to those who hear. And do not grieve the Holy Spirit of God, with which you were marked with a seal for the day of redemption. Put away from you all bitterness and wrath and anger and wrangling and slander, together with all malice, and be kind to one another, tenderhearted, forgiving one another, as God in Christ has forgiven you. Therefore be imitators of God, as beloved children, and live in love, as Christ loved us and gave himself up for us, a fragrant offering and sacrifice to God.* ⊱ Ephesians 4:29—5:2

One of the oldest priests in my home diocese would delight in telling the story of all the students in his seminary being assembled for a school picture many years ago. They stood solemnly in front of the seminary building, wearing their cassocks, while the photographer moved his primitive camera from left to right, slowly, to make one of those long, narrow photographs you sometimes see from days gone by.

Only when the picture was framed and ready to be hung in the seminary hall did anyone notice that clearly visible in the photo, leaning from an upstairs window, was one of the German nuns who had come to the States to care for the seminarians and their priest professors. Newly arrived in America, only able to speak bits of English, the nun appeared in the photo making an obscene gesture. The rector of the seminary asked the naïve sister for an explanation and was told, "The boys invited me to be in the picture. They told me that the gesture meant, 'Greetings to the student body.'"

The moral seems to be, be careful what you do or say. And where.

This moral came home to me again recently when I visited lovely Honolulu. One day there, I was asked by a priest friend to take his place at daily Eucharist. I noticed a blind man in the front pew wearing large, dark glasses, with a white cane at his side. I never saw him smile. Speaking from the pulpit about the eucharistic mystery, I quoted St. Paul: "This bread that we break, is it not the body of Christ, given for us?" (1 Corinthians 10:16).

After Mass as I entered the lobby of the building next door and moved toward the elevator, I noticed the blind man from church, glasses on and white cane tapping, making his way into the same elevator. With him was a woman who had been the reader at Mass who also lived in the building. She nodded a greeting to me, punched in his floor and her own. Just as I was about to speak, the blind man spoke. "Did you hear what that priest told us?" The woman trapped in the elevator with us flashed me a pained look. I was pretty stunned to realize that this little man did not know that I was in the ascending elevator with them.

"He told us, 'This is not the body of Christ. This is not the blood of Christ.'" I was too stunned to speak. The elevator stopped on the fifth floor, and followed by his companion wearing a weak and embarrassed smile, he tapped his way out with his white cane. The aggressor's blindness seemed to me a perfect metaphor for the other kind of blindness that might afflict us and that we might use to afflict others.

Frequent Misunderstandings

Pastoral ministers will often find themselves astonished at how misunderstood they are and how significantly what they thought that they clearly said can be misinterpreted. Perhaps it is the parish liturgist who, moments before one of the Sunday celebrations, patiently tells an inquirer that it is too late to revise the list of parish announcements in both worship locations to include news of next week's Girl Scout bake sale. That person, whom you thought you had treated kindly, fairly, and sensitively, goes off in tears to find the pastor to complain about the disrespect and humiliation she suffered. The unhappy pastor finds the confused liturgist and both of them begin Sunday's Eucharist carrying unresolved burdens. We often find ourselves wondering how we, as members of a church kissed by divinity, are captive to maddening and unmannerly behavior.

A visiting priest in a large suburban parish tells of coming to help a busy pastor who was burdened with any number of weddings and Sunday Masses on a given weekend. The visitor is no stranger there, having helped often in recent years. Usually there is a full complement of ministers to assist in any celebration, but somehow at one Saturday evening Mass there were no altar servers. Consequently there were no candles carried in procession, no candles to flank the gospel book and no candles on or near the altar during the eucharistic prayer. The visiting priest did not immediately notice their absence since usually the candles are placed by someone else.

When they had completed the celebration and he stood by the door to greet worshipers as they left, an obviously angry man came charging in his direction, shook his hand briefly, and charged on. At what he seemed to think was a safe distance, he turned back and barked, "Nice job, Father: WITHOUT the candles!" He stormed off. The priest stood, fuming silently, and watched him charge out the door. Had he not been so flummoxed by the outburst, he might have suggested that the oversight, which did not threaten the validity of what they had been about, could have been taken care of by that righteous complainer and the Eucharist could have been conducted in the proper light.

The issue here was not so much the forgotten candles, but forgotten manners. We are a church that includes some zany members, as well as folks who are sometimes hurtful in their pursuit of the gospel call as they hear it. And they are among the most wearying features of life as a pastoral minister. (The "poor" we always have with us.) Some politicians and bishops and pastors and pastoral ministers really seem to let what feels like mean-spirited criticism roll off their backs. Others of us cannot.

The week following the candle outburst, there were both servers and candles. The same man approached the same priest afterward and smiling with extended hand said with pleased relief, "You had candles this week." He projected the attitude that the problems of ministries belonged just to the visiting priest. As a worshiping (and eagle-eyed!) parishioner, he took no share of that burden other than as unmannerly critic.

Inappropriate Behavior

What is it about our current age that provokes people to think that righteous outrage is appropriate? Do they really believe that the salvation of another and the continuance of the church's mission is advanced by such behavior? The provocation caused when manners are missing, however, can either be a disruption on the spiritual path or a tool to fashion it and make it strong.

In light of international threats and violence, perhaps these concerns seem small or untimely. However, five-hundred-year-old grudges that erupt in war do not begin with mortar attacks. We must avoid even small matters of incivility if we are to build the enduring and coming reign of God. Those who see themselves as orthodox protectors of a disappearing or diminishing tradition, even in their alarm, are still obligated to behave with good manners. In the same way, those annoyed with "orthodox protectors" are also obliged to show good manners.

This is not to suggest that we should not air our differences as we seek ways to better live together and build up God's reign. But we must take seriously the challenge we hear in Ephesians: "So then, putting away falsehood, let all of us speak the truth to our neighbors, for we are members of one another. Be angry but do not sin; do not let the sun go down on your anger, and do not make room for the devil"

(Ephesians 4:25–27). Let us return again and again to the examination of our motives and our consciences day by day, seeking justice, peace, and charity but with attention to the manners we use and with attention to good manners. When we do this, we will have found our spiritual home.

Next we will consider stability, steadfastness, and holiness as important aspects of our spirituality.

For Reflection and Discussion
- Do you experience rude behavior among those you serve? How do you respond to this?
- How do you encourage the airing of differences?

PART SIX

Steadfastness

Marriage and Spirituality

*Community is presence,
not an institution.* ~ THOMAS MERTON

It takes neither a rocket scientist nor social scientist to observe how fragile is the institution of marriage in the current age. According to some estimates, divorce rates are up around forty percent, and Catholic marriages end in divorce about twenty percent of the time. Attention to the Scriptures, to the prayers and ceremony of the Rite of Marriage, and to marriage lived as sacrament in the Catholic communion provides a different vision and suggests a countercultural stance for those who look to graced love as transformative both for individuals and for society. Certainly there are tensions in every marriage and in every relationship; seeking to live a life of grace is no guarantee of a life free from stress. Learning how to live creatively and faithfully in that tension is the grace-filled goal of those who seek to live their spirituality.

In an earlier chapter, we considered the dilemma of pastoral ministers who sense that they live in fishbowls, and that their lives are not as private as they might wish. Timothy's description of the expectations of pastoral ministers makes the call to married life sound very demanding, noting that married ministers must be above reproach, temperate, sensible, respectable, hospitable, apt teachers, not drunkards, not violent but gentle, not quarrelsome, and not lovers of money, managing households well, keeping children submissive, and being respectful in every way. How, Timothy asks, can those who do not know how to manage their own households take care of God's church? (1 Timothy 3:1–5).

As statistics show and as married people will attest, marriage is not an easy vocation. The odd hours and many demands of life as a pastoral minister, as well as the problem of feeling as though one's family lives in a fishbowl, compound the difficulties. In Bobbie Ann Mason's short story "The Retreat," before Georgeann is married to Shelby Pickett, her mother warned her about the disadvantages of marrying a preacher. Though she thought Georgeann married unwisely, the mother later promotes the sanctity of the union: "Marriage is forever, but a preacher's marriage is longer than that," she says. Perhaps the burdens of marriage as well as the burdens of a more public life than one might have planned make forever seem like an even longer time than when the marriage vows were first planned or uttered.

Called to lives of virtue, pastoral ministers, in company with other married Christian people, can look to Scripture both for guidance and for challenge in building and maintaining their marriages. The life of virtue includes steadfastness and constancy, both of which are virtues that not all Christians enjoy, or even want. The gospel story of Jesus in dialogue with the Pharisees about the permanence of marriage is one that is sometimes overlooked. The Pharisees ask Jesus, as reported in Mark's gospel, if it is lawful to send away or divorce one's wife. Jesus asks what the law is, and his interlocutors refer to Deuteronomy, in which Moses seems to make divorce simple, allowing a husband to write a bill of divorce for his wife. Jesus looks to Genesis in response, citing the creation account in which God makes both male and female, noting that the two are to become one flesh (Genesis 2:24). The Jewish divorce legislation to which Jesus points seems to favor easy divorce but, as John R. Donahue, S.J., points out in his "The Word" column in *America* magazine, in practice Jewish divorce was infrequent. The teaching of Jesus was then not directed to correct widespread abuse, but to make a prophetic challenge that flows from God's creative purpose as revealed in Genesis. The challenge is to seek faithfulness, celebrate constancy, and avoid judgment while living the love of Christ. That hope is made evident in the prayer after communion in the marriage liturgy when we ask, "As you have made N. and N. / one in this sacrament of marriage / (and in the sharing of the one bread and the one cup), / so now make them one in love for each other."

The Importance of Contemplation

These are the truths and the graces we seek not just in dialogue and in shared lives but also in silence. One of the gifts of our tradition is the call to contemplation which is sometimes overlooked in the busy lives of married ministers. This is not an exercise exclusive to mountaintops, monasteries, or ashrams, however, but a staple of the Christian journey. In contemplation, we seek to open ourselves to the sanctuary within where God speaks to the human heart. It is reported that St. John Vianney, ever attentive to the transformative power of prayer, encountered an elderly man in the church one day who seemed not to pray, but sat silently, smiling. The eager pastor asked the old man why he did not pray the rosary or say the stations of the cross. The wise elder said simply, "I look at him. He looks at me. Together, we are very happy." If there were a quick course in contemplation, it would be found in his reply. Contemplation puts us on the road to holiness through wholeness and is as important for married ministers as for the ordained.

I rediscovered the importance of contemplation once in the midst of the Triduum, in the quiet of the long hours of Holy Saturday, those hours that come as solitary gift and grace to those who will keep silence even in the midst of sometimes frenzied preparation for the great Vigil. I picked up Thomas Merton's *The Springs of Contemplation: A Retreat at the Abbey of Gethsemani*, and read Merton's account of a parish priest who came to Gethsemani from a small town in Texas. His was a small, remote parish "with nobody around much"; he about fifty, "a quiet type of person." The priest expected a two-day crash course in becoming a contemplative, but was "flabbergasted" to be left alone. Merton asserts that the abbey guest house should be "for people who want to come and have silence. They shouldn't come to be talked to, but if they want, they should have somebody to talk with." The Texas priest realized right away that he could be alone and silent at home, "so he may as well have stayed where he was." Merton concludes that "there is no quick course in contemplation. It just doesn't exist. If it does, somebody's being sold a bill of goods."

Merton suggests that we must "decide where we stand and become more clear about it. That's enough. This recognition," he suggests, "is the heart of contemplative life," understanding "that you don't need any more than the real essentials." When one is "content with having met up with the essentials insofar as you can," and to "know you can't do much more than that but you've done that, is central to our life. God will take care of the rest." He points out that "suffering in the contemplative life or any religious life comes from the conviction that the action is someplace else."

Christ Is Risen

I went for a walk in rural New Hampshire to ponder all this, and strolled purposefully by a small Protestant church next to a small bank. They shared a parking lot. Apparently, pastor and banker both were fond of signs, and would-be parkers were advised that any who park, "without blessing" from bank or church "risketh towing." The church's own sign, late on a Holy Saturday afternoon when winter seemed to have changed its mind about yielding to spring, read: "Christ Has Risen." Has? The past tense? A past, completed deed? Not so! Merton asserts that to proclaim "Christ is risen and Christ lives is to mean that Christ has *really* risen and lives in us now." Always the present tense.

So it is the risen Christ, always present, ever attentive, who speaks to the silent heart. But we must recognize that silence and contemplation are choices that are open to us, and do not stand in opposition to community and certainly not to the community of marriage. Merton comments, "I'm choosing community as the place where Christ is present and acting. And he has shown this to me by the fact that these are my friends." However, "One of the things about our kind of community is that we have people among us whom we would not necessarily have picked as friends." And among friends, "Silence can be a great problem or a great grace....For too long the rule of silence was a means of being absent from one another....The justification of silence in our life is that we love one another enough to be silent together." One thinks of the Quakers, silent together in God's good presence, and also of the Christian assembly silent together as the Word and the mystery of Christ present among us are contemplated and celebrated. And, as Merton sees it, "living a contemplative, disciplined life should help us see what's artificial." Recognizing what is artificial, one ought then to see that which is real. That which is real will endure, and "the one who endures to the end will be saved" (Matthew 10:22).

All the fruits of the Christian life which feed the virtue of endurance are not clearly visible on a wedding day, or the day of enrollment in the catechumenate or of baptism, for then the adventure is just beginning. The Christian path, then, is the road to holiness through wholeness for those called to be people of peace, immersed in God's reign, striving at the invitation of Jesus to be perfected as the heavenly Father is perfect (Matthew 5:48). To have decided that this is where we stand and that here lies our hope means that we do not need more. But recognizing that we do not need more is the work of a lifetime and the goal of one who seeks the spiritual path for ministry, remembering and seeking to believe that what God said to Paul applies also to us: "My grace is sufficient for you, for power is made perfect in weakness" (2 Corinthians 12:9). Married ministers know this firsthand.

Next we will consider the importance of faith and how it can be restored and why we shouldn't give up on God.

For Reflection and Discussion

- In your opinion, how do marriage and ministry complement one another?
- What qualities from the "community" of marriage are most useful to you in your ministry?

Keeping the Faith

I have a young friend, a recent university graduate, to whom I am deeply indebted for a lesson in how faith works, falters, and rebounds. This young man is a good student, interested in many things in and out of the classroom, good-looking and affable. He spent the fall semester in eager anticipation of his girlfriend joining him at the university; she was to transfer in for the spring semester.

She arrived as planned, proved to be drop-dead gorgeous, and as smart and personable as she is beautiful. Together, they took a class from me. Their relationship was admirable. They shared a vision about an impending engagement to be followed shortly by a wedding, and their hopes, aspirations, and dreams were in view as they worked day by day through their junior year in college.

But, as sometimes happens in young love, the relationship went south midway through the semester. There seemed to be no particular cataclysm that precipitated it, no guilty or unfaithful party, just a sad parting. But young Jared suffered from the symptoms of a broken heart more egregiously than any other disappointed lover in the state of Illinois. He would come sometimes to my office to mourn, either standing silently in the doorway, head downcast, or sitting listlessly and sighing deeply. I'd tell him from time to time that "the only cure for a broken heart is the passage of time." "Yes," he'd say, "you keep saying so."

But as the semester came to its conclusion, he was not yet healed, or even healing, had failed to register for fall classes, and had lost interest in many of the things that had animated him previously. While he may not have been clinically depressed, he was deeply unhappy, and I was concerned that he might drop out of school or do something else that might be dangerous, foolish, or not in his best interest. He promised, though, to keep in touch. The semester ended and we abandoned the campus.

Jared lost faith in promises, in young love, in his beloved, in the goodness of human experience. He is, I think, a picture of what the loss of faith looks like. Writing in *America* (August 4, 2003), Sister Diane Bergant, C.S.A., points out that loss of faith does not have to do with doctrine. We do not wake up one morning doubting the Trinity or questioning the hypostatic union. She suggests that we lose faith in people to whom we had turned, or we judge that life has taken such a disastrous turn that not even God can fix it.

Giving Up on Faith

She points out that Elijah the prophet, a witness to God's mighty deeds on Mount Carmel, was cast down by the infidelity of his cohort and lost faith (1 Kings 19:4–8). Those who were miraculously fed by Jesus with loaves and fishes went away when they heard his discourse on the Bread of Life which let them know that there was more at stake than free food (John 6:41–51). They doubted the word that Jesus spoke. Living by faith, Bergant suggests, is much more difficult than studying faith. But people of faith "have to live with disappointment and loss and failure, and not give up on other people or on God."

Jared, in cooperation with God's grace, apparently came to that same insight without having read *America*. On a fine July afternoon, an e-mail message from him popped up on my computer screen. He wrote, "This summer has actually been good for me. A new perspective on life has opened up for me and I just feel much more relaxed about whatever may come my way. I am very happy with myself, just being the person I want to be. I have met up with old and new friends and am happy with life. Yesterday evening I was sitting up on my roof just looking at the sky and sunset and colors. It made me happy to be who and where I am. My view was slightly distorted by smokestacks and power lines in the distance, but I looked past those. If something is in my way I find a way around it. So that's how I am. How has your summer been?"

Jared's note could have been headlined *ad astra per aspera*, through difficulties to the stars. I am taken with the image of him on the roof at sunset, gazing into the Illinois horizon and beyond. His neighborhood has noxious elements, oil refineries, and electric transmission lines. But he can look around, through, and beyond these difficulties, delighting in the wonder and promise of God's creation, "the sky and sunset and colors."

He heard the apostle Paul's plan of action and put it to work: he no longer "grieved the Holy Spirit," but put aside bitterness, fury, and anger to live instead a life of kindness, compassion, and forgiveness (Ephesians 4:30—5:2). Bergant writes that such a choice is faith at work, strengthening us to live in a world filled with disappointment, terror, and violence, and in a church marked by betrayal and disillusionment. I am grateful to and for Jared who is a New Adam in his display of faith, trial, and resurrection. I propose that he is a model not just for one of his professors, but for pastoral ministers who work with fire, hope, and promise day by day, but who sometimes fail to appreciate the promise made through Isaiah the prophet: "a bruised reed he will not break, and a dimly burning wick he will not quench" (42:3). This suffering servant will bring justice to the nations, open the eyes of the blind, and free captives. And, reports Isaiah, "He will not fail or be discouraged" (42:4). This promise prompts perseverance.

Bergant writes in another season (*America*, January 5–12, 2004) that we Christians link Isaiah's profile of the suffering servant to Jesus, the anointed one of God. His identity and ministry are confirmed by the Spirit and the voice from heaven at his baptism (Luke 3:15–16, 21–22). She points out that the same voice stilled the chaotic waters described in Psalm 29: "The voice of the Lord is upon the waters; the God of glory thunders, the Lord, upon many waters. The voice of the Lord is powerful, the voice of the Lord is full of majesty" (3–4). She notes, too, that an ordered universe emerged out of the primeval waters to produce abundant life. Genesis reports: "The earth was without form and void, and darkness was upon the face of the deep; and the Spirit of God was moving over the face of the waters....And God made the firmament and separated the waters which were under the firmament from the waters which were above the firmament" (1:2, 7).

We Are Transformed

Bergant points to Jesus rising out of the waters of the Jordan as the one who would transform the earth. We, too, emerge from the waters of baptism, we and the waters both transformed by him. We rise up commissioned to continue the ministry Jesus began. She then sees in Acts (10:34–38) a demonstration of the fruits of the baptismal commission: Peter, representing the entire church, moves into unfamiliar realms and baptizes Cornelius and his entire gentile household. Here, Bergant finds an example of the church's universal scope. The gospel must be preached in every nation. She concludes, as we must continue to conclude, that in baptism we are all the anointed of God, "continuing what Jesus began, and doing it after the manner of the gentle servant of the Lord of whom Isaiah spoke."

Those possessed of so glorious a vocation might still suffer bruises from bumps in the road or from other travelers on the way. But the Book of Revelation delivers encouragement from the one "who holds the seven stars in his right hand, who walks among the seven golden lampstands." This one says, "I know your works, your toil, and your patient endurance." And, "I also know that you are enduring patiently and bearing up for the sake of my name, and that you have not grown weary" (2:1–3). However, he delivers a warning and a promise: "But I have this against you, that you have abandoned the love you had at first. Remember then from what you have fallen; repent, and do the works you did at first. Let anyone who has an ear listen to what the Spirit is saying to the churches. To everyone who conquers, I will give permission to eat from the tree of life that is in the paradise of

God" (4–7). Building for the reign of God is more fun and fulfilling than patient endurance. But both are essential and one supports, strengthens, and furthers the other.

As I wrote this page, my computer flashed a note indicating that an e-mail had just been delivered. At the end of it, my friend Claire had attached a piece of Psalm 145, and I was glad to be reminded that "The Lord is faithful in all his words, and gracious in all his deeds. The Lord upholds all who are falling, and raises up all who are bowed down" (13–14). The psalmist reminds God in order to remind us: "The eyes of all look hopefully to you, O Lord, and you give them their food in due season. You open your hand, and fill your creature world with blessing" (15–16).

Grace, which is everywhere, is designed to prompt hearts in gratitude. The practice of cultivating both grace and gratitude, which is clearly the call of a eucharistic people (and certainly the call of all in pastoral ministry!), will ease anxiety, combat stress, provoke hopefulness, and keep charity in focus. Still, some among us worry that our good efforts might be quietly extinguished or somehow diminished. Some fear that they may lose heart. Others are concerned that their early love may falter and perhaps die. We might reclaim a prayer in loose translation from the Missal of Pius V: "Have mercy on your people, Lord, and give us / a breathing space in the midst of so many troubles."

The enduring faith of the eucharistic communion assures us that we will not lose heart, reforms will not be undone, the church will not wither, and the one "who began a good work in you will bring it to completion at the day of Jesus Christ" (Philippians 1:6).

There is no desert whose dust will choke the coming reign of God. We persevere in prayer, guided again by the psalmist:

> *When they asked for food he sent quails;*
> *He filled them with bread from heaven.*
> *He pierced the rock to give them water;*
> *It gushed forth in the desert like a river.*

For he remembered his holy word,
Which he gave to Abraham his servant.
So he brought out his people with joy,
His chosen ones with shouts of rejoicing (105).

We who walk by faith will not be free from disappointment, but neither will we perish or lose hope. Even in a church scarred and stained, even for pastoral ministers who are sometimes weary or discouraged, the eucharistic table keeps the light alive and the path open. Those who seek the spiritual path will say, "Thanks be to God."

Next we will consider extending the hand of Jesus as an exercise in compassion and solidarity, one that promotes growth in others, in the body of Christ, and in our own spiritual journey.

For Reflection and Discussion

- In what ways have you experienced ministry as *ad astra per aspera* (through difficulties to the stars)?
- What keeps you from becoming weary or discouraged? How do you help others to find a "breathing space in the midst of so many troubles"?

Serving One Another

Jesus said to them, "There is no need for them to go away; give them some food yourselves."
≈ Matthew 14:16

I arranged to go on an expedition with one of my nephews one August day in preparation for his entry into first grade. I had expected to buy some school supplies, and was not prepared to learn a lesson in how one ministers, much less see a demonstration of how a spiritual path unfolds even in a retail outlet. Young Brandon and I went off to the Target store near his home and chose first a backpack, then a lunch box, pencils (no pens in first grade!), a large eraser, a notebook, folders, crayons, felt-tipped markers, and then a shirt and pair of slacks. He arranged everything in the cart just so, and transferred everything carefully to the counter when we made our way to the checkout.

He politely waited until it was our turn, and then announced good news of great joy to the young cashier, "These are my things! And I am going to be a first-grader!"

The cashier appeared to be a high school student, and on a busy summer afternoon might not have cared particularly about her small customer's September destination. But this young woman was uncommonly filled with both grace and wisdom, and she replied enthusiastically, observing that he had all the supplies he needed, seemed very well prepared, and was sure to be successful. He smiled broadly and nodded his agreement and his thanks.

I had just visited a friend before we went to shop, and he had prominently displayed an icon of Peter, having failed to walk on the water, taking the outstretched hand of Jesus. But here before me in the checkout lane of a suburban Target was a new icon, the same scene, but with new faces. Peter was a small boy stepping out on his excellent adventure, and Jesus was a blond behind a cash register in a red Target polo shirt. I had not gone to Target expecting to see the face of God, but such surprises are consistent with our tradition. Elijah the prophet looked in all the wrong places, failing to find God in the strong and heavy wind, or in the fire, or in the earthquake, but unexpectedly in a tiny whispering sound.

Serving One Another

I remembered Matthew's account of Jesus about to feed the vast crowd (14:13–21). The disciples wanted to send everyone away to find something for themselves to eat. "You give them something to eat," said Jesus. Here is an important moment in the development of our eucharistic theology: It is not just what God does for us that brings about God's reign; it is also what we do one for another. If my young nephew is always surrounded and supported by family and friends who encourage him, assure him of his possibilities, buoy him up, challenging him and cheering him on, he is sure to be successful in all he attempts, and thus will God's will be done, and the kingdom come. All of our children and, indeed, all of us, deserve nothing less.

I could not help but contrast that grace-filled moment with an encounter I had the previous Sunday after one of the Masses in the parish where I assisted in the summer months. A man approached me and asked, "Do you know what you should do?" I understood immediately that by "you" he meant "youse," not just me, but the pastor, and all American priests with whom we should shortly be in contact to share the mission on which we were about to be sent.

When someone whose name I do not know asks me, "Do you know what you should do?" my first impulse is to say, "Yes, I do know what I should do. I should not listen to what you are about to say." I did not say that, but did listen, and he told me that we priests should tell the rest of Catholic people that whatever may ail the church, we should stick together, and not lose faith, and keep our eyes and minds on what is most important. That exact idea had been the constant theme of my preaching all summer long. How had he missed that? No "Good Listener Award" for him! Further, just thirty minutes earlier, he had heard his pastor develop (and rather brilliantly, I thought) the idea that it is not just what God does for us, but what we do for each other that will bring about the progress and healing of peoples: "You give them something to eat."

If our attitude is that the priests should hop to and get it done (whatever it is at the moment), or if we think a crisp one-dollar bill in the basket is the key, we have missed hearing the gospel, we have failed to extend the hand that is not just ours, but is the very hand of the healing, saving Christ. The fellow who wanted to send me off to do what needed to be done was justifiably concerned. And he was certainly correct about the fact that in the boat, the church, the wind will die down, and we are where we ought to be, and there we will be safe, and there we will meet the Lord. But to get to the boat, to recognize it as the place where we belong, we often need the extended hand that belongs both to Jesus and to each of us. My model that day, in fact shipmate of the week, was the young clerk at Target; may she live long and prosper; may all those she encourages flourish; may God's kingdom come, and God's will be done on earth as it is in heaven.

Next we consider what we learn about the spiritual path from burying a pope and studying the funeral liturgy.

For Reflection and Discussion

- Are there people in your ministry whom you experience as "uncommonly filled with both grace and wisdom"? How do such people help you?
- How do you respond to those who misinterpret or completely miss your message? What keeps you going in the face of such discouragement?

PART SEVEN

Ritual as Teacher

The Burial of a Pope

*Those who do what is true come to the light,
so that it may be clearly seen that their deeds
have been done in God.* ~ JOHN 3:21

I was awestruck by the outpouring of emotion and the torrent of information, both news and features, when the Catholic world buried Karol Wojtyla who served the church as Pope John Paul II for twenty-six years. There were reports of millions of people attempting to squeeze themselves into the St. Peter's Square which holds only eight hundred thousand. My hometown newspaper, the "Duluth News Tribune," opened its Web site, inviting people to share feelings and post condolences. All of this gave testimony to the fact that something most unusual was happening in human hearts. Reflecting on that experience will school the pastoral minister in the dual significance of our ritual as agent of God's transforming presence to the church, as well as liturgy's gift of explicating the church's teaching both in what we say and what we do.

The next generation of scholars, including theologians, sociologists, and historians, will have the task of examining and interpreting the phenomena of the days and years of John Paul's pontificate. For Catholic people, the first task was to be attentive to what the church prays at the time of death and burial and continues to pray in the nine official days of mourning, and then to continue to ponder the deeper meaning of our prayers and beliefs as time moves on. An important Catholic principle helps make sense of what the church at prayer is about in the burial of a pope or any other person: *lex orandi, lex credendi*—the law of prayer establishes the law of belief, which is to say that the church's prayer establishes and reveals what the church believes.

The Memory of Baptism

The funeral rite both for the pope and any Catholic person begins by evoking the memory of baptism: "On the day of his baptism, Karol Wojtyla put on Christ. In the day of Christ's coming, may he be clothed in glory." This prayer illustrates the sure and certain hope of Christian people that those who have spent their lives in service of God by serving humankind will be forgiven their sins and share in the glory of Christ's resurrection. The first and greatest dignity for any Christian, pope, or person in the back pew, comes in being claimed in baptism as a child of God born again in water and the Holy Spirit.

The funeral prayers make it explicit that we do not canonize the dead as saints on the day of their burial: Judgment is left to God; and, proclamations of sanctity are left for a later date. It is presumed that all of us have sinned and have fallen short of perfection. We pray for each of those we bury that God will "forgive whatever sins he [or she] may have committed." The hymn "Amazing Grace" repeats this theme by reminding us that "Grace will lead [us] home."

One of the prayers that begins the funeral of a pope asks God: "In your mercy bring him with the flock entrusted to his care / to the reward you have promised your faithful servants." The faithful servants include not just popes, bishops, and hierarchy; the faithful are the people of God among whom the pope is numbered. What may be his finest title, Servant of the Servants of God, expresses this idea of his place among us as one who serves.

An open book of the gospels is usually placed on a bishop's closed casket (remember that the pope is the Bishop of Rome), over his face, to suggest that this Christian lived under the gospel of Christ. The open book also calls to mind the book of the gospels which is held by two deacons tentlike over a man's head when he is ordained a bishop, a reminder and promise to live under the gospel day by day and decision by decision.

Catholic people are usually buried from a church building. The idea is that they have been nourished Sunday by Sunday at the eucharistic table, which points to and connects with the banquet table set in readiness for us in the kingdom of heaven. The pope's funeral was outside, in front of St. Peter's, to accommodate the larger crowd but the idea is clearly evident that the Eucharist celebrated in the presence of his body is the foretaste and promise of the heavenly banquet. The prayer after communion asks: "Lord, / at this meal of eternal life / we ask for your mercy for your servant John Paul. / May he rejoice forever in the possession of that truth / in which he made your people strong by faith."

Perhaps the finest epitaph for John Paul II and any Christian might be found in John's gospel (3:21): "He who does what is true comes to the light, that it may be clearly seen that his deeds have been wrought in God." May all of us who seek to minister find both challenge and guidance in that verse.

Next we will consider what we learn by examining and praying the funeral liturgy and we will focus on what it says about grief and hope.

For Reflection and Discussion

- In what ways are you a "servant of the servants of God"?
- What words or example from John Paul II has touched your own life and ministry?

Burdens Lifted

O God,
in whom sinners find mercy and
*   the saints find joy,*
we pray to you for our brother [sister] N.,
whose body we honor with Christian burial,
that he [she] may be delivered
*   from the bonds of death.*
Admit him [her] to the joyful company
*   of your saints*
and raise him [her] on the last day
to rejoice in your presence forever.
We ask this through our Lord Jesus Christ,
*   your Son,*
who lives and reigns with you and the Holy Spirit,
one God for ever and ever.
*   Amen.*   ❧ Funeral Mass, Opening Prayer C

We in pastoral ministry are perhaps more aware than others of the power of ritual and liturgy to accomplish within us what we alone cannot. I was called not long ago when a young friend went down in a tiny aircraft on the foggy shore of Lake Superior. She was with her two daughters, three and four, and her brother-in-law, the pilot. The mother and the pilot died on impact and the babies wandered in the woods, burned and frightened, for several hours before their rescue. At her funeral some days later, I would not have wanted to depend on my eloquence or understanding of providence and grace to make sense of this tragedy as the young widower sat in the front pew flanked by his own and her grieving parents, their siblings, the four year old in a tiny wheelchair, the large congregation stunned and in sorrow.

We did not know why this young wife and mother died, but our ritual and prayer affirmed for us why she lived, and our belief in the communion of saints gave us hope. God's glory was revealed in her: we who were touched in and by her brief life were schooled in the Spirit's gift of awe and wonder; we experienced the transforming power of love; we saw kindness at work and gentleness at play. The Incarnate Christ lived in her, and she in Christ. We glimpsed mystery and God among us. And in the face of this great gift, we blessed the Lord and gave our thanks.

When the Sacred Congregation for Divine Worship issued the *Rite of Funerals*, revised by Decree of the Second Vatican Council and published by the authority of Pope Paul VI in 1969, it noted that the church's funeral custom has been not only to commend the dead to God but also to support Christian hope in its people and give witness to its faith in the future resurrection of the baptized with Christ.

This important piece of Christian practice and teaching sometimes seems lost in modern obituary pages where it is often reported that "at the deceased's request, there will be no services." Anecdotal reports from pastors and funeral directors suggest that this is a mistake on several levels, and that mourning and ritual are important both to individuals and to families as well as to the larger community and to the body of Christ. Even "Dominick Dunne's Diary" in *Vanity Fair* (July 2005) laments "I hate it when friends leave strict instructions before they die that there is to be no funeral or memorial service. I've always been a big funeral-goer and a firm believer that surviving friends and relatives need an occasion to be with all the other people who miss the departed the same way they do. You want to hug one another and share stories about the person you all cared about." Dunne seems to agree with St. Augustine who writes that "All these things—the care of the funeral arrangements, the establishment of the place of burial, the pomp of the ceremonies—are more of a solace for the living than an aid for the dead" ("On the Care for the Dead"). The church intercedes for the dead "because of its confident belief that death is not the end nor does it break the bonds forged in life." In addition, "The church also ministers to the sorrowing and consoles them in the funeral rites with the comforting word of God and the sacrament of the Eucharist" (*Rite of Funerals*, General Introduction, 4).

A community gathers around the body of a loved one, making rituals, repeating certain words, singing psalms, hymns, and inspired songs, calling upon God to affirm that love is stronger than death. The Christian community invokes the presence of Jesus risen from the dead, the first fruits of a new creation that ends not in death but in glory. The message to us is that God invites us to divine life as the perfection of our human journey.

A funeral ritual that fails to affirm this hope is a burden on top of grief, even if it is a fine, feel-good moment in which a human life is remembered and projected into a heaven where dead people now look down on us and smile or play golf with God. The paschal mystery is more than this, and a well celebrated funeral with powerful preaching invites people to live the mystery now, more generously, ready to risk all because they no longer fear death.

Good ritual makes all of this clear. The reception and opening of the casket, and the closing of the casket in farewell, the music and prayers, the symbols of light, water, the white pall, the Scripture selections, the homily, the core action of the eucharistic liturgy, communion, commissioning—all of this conveys powerfully, often to a group of people whose relationship to religion is peripheral, the gospel of Life with all its implications for how the living go forth from church, the cemetery, back into their lives. To be unprepared for or to squander this moment for any reason is to deny people the hope they were promised by the community at baptism.

Divine Mystery

We buried a federal judge recently, a mighty pillar of the local church and an exemplar as a servant of the law. As we sang the judge to his grave, as we brought his body up the hill for burial in sure hope of resurrection, we struggled with the mystery of life and death, with the threat and the promise of our own mortality. Consoling his family, we consoled ourselves by remembering this man of great integrity, celebrating his many virtues which enhanced life for his family, for us, and for our community. But if we are truly to remember him, if we really mourn his passing, if we hope to meet again, we must cherish those whom he loved, recount those things he taught us, revere the institutions he revered, and imitate the love that quickened him, thus ensuring his continued memory in our midst. All of this becomes clear in the unfolding liturgy, the public reading of the transforming Word, and the celebration of the Eucharist.

The ritual well done is itself a kind of structure for the human process of grief, enabling the bereaved to accept the fact of death but then guiding them to hope. The homily is a chance to explicate this progress toward faith, but the ritual itself possesses a genius for accomplishing the actual catechesis. A good presider goes with the ritual's flow. And the ritual makes clear what its General Introduction stresses: "The community's principal involvement in the ministry of consolation is expressed in its active participation in the celebration of the funeral rites, particularly the vigil for the deceased, the funeral liturgy, and the rite of committal" (11). An initial pastoral visit to a family after a loved one's death is important as the first tangible expression of the community's support for those who mourn. Additionally, "A minister unfamiliar with the family or the deceased person can learn a great deal on this occasion about the needs of the family and the life of the deceased" (103). Parish leaders are invited to involve the family in planning the funeral rites and to encourage family members to take an active part in the ministries at the various celebrations, though "they should not be asked to assume any role that their grief or sense of loss may make too burdensome" (15).

Throughout all the rites leading to the grave, Scripture provides both comfort and direction: "The readings proclaim to the assembly the paschal mystery, teach remembrance of the dead, convey the hope of being gathered together again in God's kingdom, and encourage the witness of Christian life." And, above all, "tell of God's designs for a world in which suffering and death will relinquish their hold on all whom God has called his own" (22).

The ritual also clearly states that a brief homily based on the readings should be given after the gospel reading and may also be given after the readings at the vigil service. The homilist is to be attentive to the grief of those present, dwelling on God's compassionate love and on the paschal mystery. The homilist is encouraged to help the members of the assembly understand that the mystery of God's love and the mystery of Jesus' death and resurrection were present in the life and death of the deceased and that these mysteries are active in their own lives too. The homily thus provides both consolation and strength to face death with hope. Priests often point out that priests themselves often violate this charge when burying their brother priests.

We often see the gospel writ large in the lives of the faithful we bury and do well to make those homiletic references. But canonization must be left for a later date. We gather to pray that God will forgive whatever sins the deceased may have committed; we do not announce her or his arrival in heaven. To do so is inappropriate on many levels, usurping God's authority and presuming a knowledge known to God alone. A quick canonization is dangerous business because it overlooks the human flaws which all of us have. Plaster of Paris saints do not have such flaws. If we rush to sainthood and into plaster those who have gone before us, the real danger is that we will not call ourselves to measure up to them, excusing ourselves from duty because saints are saints and we are but flesh and blood.

But this immediate canonization is less likely to happen if the family has other opportunities—perhaps as part of the vigil—to tell stories, laugh, cry. For most families, this needs to happen somewhere, and most understand that this important and personal expression of memory, grief, and hope really should not infiltrate the liturgy which is larger than the individual being buried. The vigil is an opportunity for the gathered family and friends to rejoice in their memories: At the vigil or wake the Christian community keeps watch with the family as they pray to the God of mercy and find strength in Christ's presence.

The young mother mentioned at the beginning of the chapter was well and lovingly remembered by a procession of family, friends, colleagues, and neighbors. This gathering went on as long as those present needed to continue. Those with other obligations, or who tired out more quickly, were free to leave at a time they chose. This approach honors those who wish to speak but leaves the funeral Mass unencumbered with eulogies and remembrances. Part of the genius of the Roman Rite is that it is spare; simplicity, truth, and beauty are reflected and celebrated through it.

The Liturgy Is Key

One recent week as our local priests were preparing for clergy moves and many were off on vacation, I was called to preside at a funeral of someone I did not know. I felt no apprehension, and apparently, neither did the grieving family. The ritual and the Word of God were both far more important than whether or not the presider and preacher had been personally acquainted with the deceased or the grieving.

The ritual includes receiving the body at the door of the church. It seems curious, I think, for the hearse and family to arrive and wait there for the priest to come in procession down the aisle. The rite (133) certainly seems to leave room for the priest and ministers to be waiting at the door to welcome the family and receive the body. Many churches have baptismal fonts near the door and it certainly seems powerful to scoop water from the font for the blessing of the body rather than employing an aspergillum (a container for sprinkling holy water). I invited the family to join in this ritual, dipping their hands into the font and signing the casket, and they were pleased to do so. They joined me then in placing the pall on the casket as another reminder of baptismal dignity and the promises it brings.

A Unique Gathering

Any pastoral minister recognizes that the congregation assembled for any particular funeral is a congregation that will probably never be assembled again. Some are family members from distant places, some are neighbors, and often only a few members of the local parish are present. Here is an evangelical opportunity in which the ritual itself, lovingly celebrated, invites awe and teaches what the church understands in celebrating the sacred mysteries. One who listens carefully to the funeral prayers will go away with an enriched understanding of how Christians view death. I recently attended a funeral in a large and lovely suburban church, and the presider, not on fire either with charisma or a special flair for preaching, attended carefully to prayer and ritual, genuinely welcomed all who were in attendance, welcomed and clearly appreciated the ministries of the many parishioners assisting in the liturgy as greeters, ushers, ministers of word and music. The clear, unspoken consensus of the assembly was that the dead woman was reverently buried and the church's riches were evident and consoling. Those who wished a deeper understanding of the mysteries were well schooled by the unfolding liturgy.

Sure and Certain Hope

Priests, deacons, and all who minister in the context of the funeral liturgy do well to read, and reread often, the *General Instructions for the Funeral Liturgy*. They are rich and instructive. Some presiders, for example, are surprised to note that the liturgy ends not at the altar but at the grave, and in their confusion give a blessing while still in church and utter a dismissal even though the rite clearly does not call for it then. Clearly, they really are not dismissing the assembly at this point, but inviting them to make procession to the cemetery where the liturgy will end and where a blessing is given. Such mistakes can be avoided by careful consideration of the instructions. "Rubrics" really is not a dirty word, and these carefully worded directions give dignity to the celebration of the mysteries.

Attentive to what we believe, pray, and celebrate, we can walk from the grave "in the sure and certain hope that, together with all who have died in Christ" (Prayer of Commendation, 202), we will rise on the last day. We in pastoral ministry are called not just to believe this, but to study and teach it so that we and those to whom we minister might be transformed by its truth.

Next we will consider "crisis" as opportunity to grow spirituality and to reach out to others.

For Reflection and Discussion

- What ideas from these reflections support you in your own ministry?
- In what ways does your ministry offer others a "sure and certain hope"? How might you do this better?

PART EIGHT

Seeking Clarity

Contemporary Issues

Lord God,
protector and ruler of your church,
fill your servants with a spirit of understanding,
   truth, and peace.
Help them to strive with all their hearts
to learn what is pleasing to you,
and to follow it with all their strength.
        ❧ OPENING PRAYER,
     MASS FOR A COUNCIL OR SYNOD

There are tensions in our lives, ministries, and church that are not of our making, but which both inform and complicate our lives and ministries. As we seek understanding and peace, it is often evident that we need assistance. It is also evident, at least to me, that we teachers, pastors, and pastoral workers need some teaching ourselves if we are to continue effectively both in ministry and in forming and living our spiritualities. At least I do. Of special concern is Pope John Paul II's insistence, in *Ordinatio sacerdotalis,* that the church "has no authority whatsoever to confer priestly ordination on women." And "this judgment is to be definitively held by all the faithful." The discussion is closed. Obediently, bishops, theologians, and pastoral ministers have ceased public discussion and dialogue. The Catholic folks, however, have not ceased their unofficial discussions. And this complicates the lives and spiritual journeys of those in ministry, especially women and those attentive to their developing roles. Understanding what is at issue is essential for those in ministry.

Even after John Paul's pronouncement, there is no unanimity of opinion on the matter of whether the church has authority to confer priestly ordination on women. Polls, however, continue to indicate that more and more American people favor the ordination of women as priests. Even though most recognize that the church is not and will not be a democracy and that the sense of the faithful is not made evident even by the best secular pollsters, it seems clear that the church faces either a crisis or an opportunity, and either way, the bishops are called to act and teach quickly. We in ministry have a special obligation here; I hope that I can explain that obligation in faithfulness to our tradition of honest exploration while remaining obedient to the directives of *Ordinatio sacerdotalis* which are still in force. We must seek to understand what and why the church teaches about holy orders.

The Sense of the Faithful

Cardinal Avery Dulles asserts that the sense of the faithful is not forged in the media. It is clear that not all reporters understand the nuances of theological thought. Reporters can report on what they hear from Catholic people, but if ordinary Catholics learn most of what they know about intrachurch debate and dialogue from the secular media, can there be a sense of the faithful formed this way? How can we ascertain the sense of the faithful in this electronic age of instantaneous communication? Even if some would suggest that the assent of the faithful is no longer necessary before doctrine is promulgated, it would certainly seem evident that if we are to live peaceably in one church, that which is asserted as true and binding has to be explained in a manner accessible both to the church's pastors and theologians, as well as to the folks in the pews. There is a very certain burden here. That burden seems to rest squarely on the shoulders of the bishops. They might wish to remember Cardinal John Henry Newman's cautionary conclusion to "On Consulting the Faithful in Matters of Doctrine": the church will be happier with her enthusiastic partisans about her than if she cuts off the faithful from the study of her divine doctrines and simply requires faith. Such a requirement, he warns, "in the educated classes will terminate in indifference, and in the poorer in superstition."

John Paul also asserts that the issue of ordination is not one of justice. The reasons for this are not immediately clear. It is clear that the church's tradition, long if not unbroken, is to reserve ordination to men alone. If that is the will of God, and if the intercessory prayers of the Roman breviary when next revised continue to ask God to "call men to serve at your altar," rather than to "call those whom you choose," then we teachers need authoritative help to enable us to be credible teachers. The church is and can be countercultural, so society's pressure will not decide the issue, but in the church's grand tradition, justice will triumph eventually. The fact that the church will do what is right and just is not the issue here. Justice is always the aim and the first virtue of development. What is immediately at issue is the need for a convincing explanation of why we are to hold definitively that women cannot be ordained and why it is not a matter of justice.

Seeking justice is laudable; agreeing on what is just is not always so easy. For example, the gospel calls for work in favor of the poor and oppressed. The preferential option for the poor flows out of the prophetic song of the Magnificat and the challenge of the Beatitudes. It is clear that God wills the progress of peoples with liberty and justice for all. This stance is easy to comprehend even if not easily accomplished, and in this assertion, the church is countercultural, standing against oppressive cultures and agents of tyranny as well as tyranny itself. In the gospel's light, greed is doomed and conspicuous consumerism is at least suspect. Those who read the gospel can certainly disagree on how to arrive at liberty and justice for all, and here perhaps is the church's wisdom in standing outside as critic and provocateur rather than managing civil governments and having priests serve as legislators and bishops as prime ministers.

It is clear as well that it is the will of God revealed in the command of Christ that the church gather in his memory and be transformed by his Real Presence. The church has been always faithful here, as the *Constitution on the Sacred Liturgy* so poetically notes: "The church has never failed to come together to celebrate the paschal mystery...'giving thanks to God for his inexpressible gift' in Christ Jesus 'in praise of his glory' through the power of the Holy Spirit" (6). How Christ is present has not changed, but the church's perception and description of that presence has developed over the years. William C. Placher's *A History of Christian Thought* is helpful in charting this development: a Council of the Eastern church at Nicaea in 787 affirmed the eucharistic Real Presence, but in the next century, the French theologian Paschasius Radbertus asserted that the eucharistic bread and wine ceased to be bread and wine, becoming instead the body and blood of Christ and, in fact, the same body that was born in the manger and later died on Calvary. Radbertus, in defending the virgin birth, also suggested that just as the risen Christ passed through closed doors, so also did the baby Jesus pass miraculously through his mother's womb.

Radbertus's contemporary, Ratramnus, said such a birth would be a monstrosity, and that the vision of the Eucharist was vulgar literalism. He appealed to St. Augustine's authority in suggesting that the body of Christ is a divine reality which is not visibly present. Some two hundred years later, the idea was advanced that the bread and wine stop being bread and wine and become instead the body and blood of Christ. The words of the eucharistic prayers and the principle of *lex orandi, lex credendi* support this understanding of what happens in the Eucharist. Aristotelian terminology calls the process transubstantiation, and the Fourth Lateran Council declared it doctrinal in 1215.

Isn't it interesting that for over half the church's lifetime, how Christ was present in the Eucharist was not articulated? The fact that he was present, really and substantially, was evident, celebrated, and sufficient. The articulation of how Christ was present seemed less urgent a question than the continued celebration of that transforming presence. While some lay people today might not be able to express their belief in the Real Presence in language that will ring with theological precision, Catholics do believe that Christ is really present in the Eucharist (see "Is Jesus Really There? Most Catholics still agree," by James D. Davidson in *Commonweal*, Oct. 12, 2001). That teaching continues to have a ringing endorsement by the faithful.

Who Is Called?

Perhaps a similar development is underway with regard to the rightful place of women in the church and a developing sense of how the sacrament of orders serves the church and who can and ought be called to orders. The pattern of male dominance in church and society has been so entrenched over the centuries that any discussion of a developing role for women is a relatively recent phenomenon. Feminists can celebrate Maine's Senator Margaret Chase Smith, the first woman to serve in both the U.S. House and Senate, whose political career spanned more than three decades from 1940–1973. However, as we look at a still predominately male House and Senate, Senator Smith seems not so much someone who inaugurated a new era, but a pioneer in a yet untamed frontier (even when California's Representative Nancy Pelosi became Speaker of the House of Representatives).

It is clear that the church, at least since Vatican II, supports such progress. Speaking to the "Broader aspirations of man[sic]kind," The Church in the Modern World observes approvingly that "women claim parity with men in fact as well as of rights, where they have not already obtained it" (GS 9). Further, "At all times the church carries the responsibility of reading the signs of the time and of interpreting them in the light of the gospel, if it is to carry out its task" (4). And, significantly, "At present women are involved in nearly all spheres of life: they ought to be permitted to play their part fully according to their own particular nature. It is up to everyone to see to it that women's specific and necessary participation in cultural life be acknowledged and fostered" (60). It is clear that the church calls for and supports the progress of women as part and parcel of the progress of peoples.

What is not clear is how the church reconciles these progressive assertions with the fact that authority in the church seems reserved for those in orders and orders exclusively for males. Theologians have not been able to explain this in a convincing way. In a recent doctoral dissertation published as *The Trinitarian Foundation of Human Sexuality as Revealed by Christ According to Hans Urs von Balthasar: The Revelatory Significance of the Male Christ and the Male Ministerial Priesthood*, Robert A. Pesarchick, a priest of the archdiocese of Philadelphia, points to Hans Urs von Balthasar (1905–88), the estimable Swiss theologian, and his conviction that the reservation of priestly ordination to baptized males is intrinsically connected to the significance of the maleness of Christ himself. In *Thoughts on the Priesthood of Women*, von Balthasar writes, "For just as the Son makes present the Father's authority in the world, the Son cannot be present in the church without the aspect of chistological authority, which, because the Son represents the Father as male, can fall in an organic way only to men." Pesarchick admits that "in no work in particular, however, does von Balthasar present in a sustained, systematic, and detailed manner the reasoning and various elements that underlie his position in these matters. This is specifically true in regard to his position on the maleness of Christ and its connection to the reservation of priestly ordination to males."

So here, it seems, is the agenda. Perhaps it is the will of God that the male Christ continue to preside at the eucharistic table through the ministry of male priests. If it is God's will, it must be the practice of the church. The church then has a serious duty not to make the teaching palatable, but to make it comprehensible and convincing. Von Balthasar left the task unfinished; no one else seems to have either attempted or accomplished it in a way that will invite a final and authoritative conciliar statement that will be as happily accepted as the Fourth Lateran Council's 1215 declaration on the eucharistic presence of Christ.

In "An Essay on the Development of Christian Doctrine," Newman asserts that the more claim an idea has to be considered living, the more various will be its aspects. The more social and political its nature, the more complicated and subtle will be its development. By way of illustration, he suggests that inspired documents, such as Scripture, were intended to create an idea, which is not in the sacred text, but in the mind of the reader. "The question is, whether that idea is communicated to him in its completeness and minute accuracy, on its first apprehension, or expands in his heart and intellect, and comes to perfection in the course of time" (Chapter II, I, I). Is the teaching of *Ordinatio sacerdotalis* a doctrine, the subtlety of which will have to expand in our hearts and intellects, with a more perfect understanding to follow? If so, perhaps the suggestion that women ought to be called to orders is every bit as silly as the notion that Jesus passed through the Virgin's womb as smoke through gauze, or as odd as the assertion that the eucharistic species is a presence no different from the swaddled babe or crucified Jesus. The bishops, shepherds, and chief teachers, should be prodded to consider that the electronic age is facilitating a discussion forbidden to theologians but much underway among the faithful. While an earlier and more leisurely age allowed discussion to be carried on over hundreds of years, it should also be noted that not only was there no e-mail, but most folks could not read, and some of the clergy weren't so good at it themselves. Even most of those who were good readers did not have ready access to journals and libraries. Never before anywhere on earth has there been so large and well educated a church as lives and moves and has its being in the current age in these United States. Even if not as well educated in theology as in other disciplines, this developing church seeks an explanation of our current practice and long tradition with regard to reserving holy orders to males alone.

The Congregation for the Doctrine of the Faith holds that the teaching of *Ordinatio sacerdatolis* requires definitive assent and that it in some way pertains to the deposit of faith. Further, the teaching does not belong to matters freely open to dispute and requires the definitive assent of the faithful. Bishops are clearly in agreement; those who have reservations or who are in any way hesitant are not promoted to the episcopacy. In the interest of holding the church together, we must petition our bishops to teach us how to be as confident as they are about the rightness of this papal assertion. It would be disrespectful both of them and their authority and of all God's people to suggest that there is some special *gnosis* to which people outside the fullness of holy orders have no access. The cry of the people is urgent, and the hemorrhaging of both women and men from the church continues with no end in sight. If the bishops truly regard the teaching in *Ordinatio sacerdotalis* as irreformable, and we can only interpret their silence as consent, then we teachers need some help here in explaining how it is God's will. Doing God's will with good cheer and in good faith is clearly the aim and honest desire of all Catholic people. Is it not the task today of all in pastoral ministry to petition our bishops to make the church's teaching clear, and to invite Catholic people of good will and on both sides of the issue to join in that respectful request?

Next we will consider our duty to perform our ministry as instructed by Jesus and the church.

For Reflection and Discussion
- How would you explain "sensus fidelum" if asked?
- What is your own attitude toward *Ordinatio sacerdotalis*? How might you explain its teaching?

The Eucharist and the Church

The active role of the laity is not to be overshadowed, forgotten, relegated to insignificance, or confused with spectatorship.

Is any sentence from the documents of Vatican II quoted more often that Paragraph 14 of the *Constitution on the Sacred Liturgy* (SC): "[A]ll the faithful should be led to full, conscious, and active participation" in the liturgy? Such participation, the Constitution continues, "by the Christian people as 'a chosen race, a royal priesthood, a holy nation, a redeemed people' (1 Peter 2:9; cf. 2:4–5), is their right and duty by reason of their baptism."

Even in a church baffled and befuddled by sinfulness, we in pastoral ministry together with all Catholics today can rejoice to note that "The church has never failed to come together to celebrate the paschal mystery…'giving thanks to God for his inexpressible gift' in Christ Jesus 'in praise of his glory' through the power of the Holy Spirit" (SC 6). Since the moment the command was heard from the lips of Jesus, "Do this in remembrance of me" (Luke 22:19), the breaking of the bread and sharing of the cup has been central to the life of the church. That action makes and keeps us church. We are not free to invent a substitute or to find alternatives. We in pastoral ministry, well aware that the Eucharist makes the church even as the church makes Eucharist, must make it our mission to keep this truth in focus even if it sometimes seems that some others, including, sadly, our bishops, lose that focus. Surely this task is the special focus of all lay ministers, and, as noted in previous chapters, the key to developing a spirituality that works.

In my estimation, it is rare that our bishops have ever been as bold as they have been in proposing a new way to keep the Lord's day: without the Eucharist. Surely "Sunday Celebrations in the Absence of a Priest" (from the Bishops' Committee on the Liturgy in accordance with the Directory issued from Rome's Sacred Congregation for the Sacraments and Divine Worship) is even more radical than anything Martin Luther had in mind as he invited discussion of his ninety-five theses. As Luther moved toward Augsburg, he reformed the celebration of the Eucharist to include communion in the hand and from the cup, prayed in German, and inviting extensive lay participation in sacred song, thus anticipating Vatican II's eventual reforms. He would certainly have considered the current preparation for Eucharist-less Sundays as one more outrage. So should modern faithful Catholics, I think. It is the special task of all of us in pastoral ministry to guide this discussion.

The bishops who implement "Sunday Celebrations in the Absence of a Priest" are a more liberal and dangerous group, I think, than any on the horizon, seemingly ready to sacrifice the sacramental life of the assembly as they prepare to Protestant-ize the church in a way that did not occur to Luther. The plan threatens to reduce the church to one of Word alone rather than the Word and Sacrament that has been both source and summit since Jesus entered the upper room with his disciples and transformed the Passover for Christians in every age. What can the bishops be thinking? How is it that the command of Jesus, which has nourished the church in every age, is replaced by a new service?

The Eucharist is central to life in the church. A prayer from the *Leonine Sacramentary* (from the era of Pope St. Leo, 440–61, who may or may not have written some of the prayers) notes that "As often as the commemoration of this sacrifice is celebrated, the work of our redemption is carried out" (GIRM 2; see also "Evening Mass of the Lord's Supper," prayer over the offerings). Sundays without the Eucharist would place us in a gravely dangerous situation. While growing numbers of Catholic people in the United States are served by a diminishing number of priests, the church's law is that Catholic people have the right to the sacraments. It is not a privilege that the hierarchy makes available, but a sacred duty imposed on bishops, obliging them to provide priests for the communities under their care.

This law, it seems to me, imposes duties and obligations not just on bishops, but also on all Catholic people who are to seek priests to serve them in this age of collaborative ministry. In this age, we are still not entirely sure what John XXIII meant in *Pacem in Terris*: "Those who discover that they have rights have the responsibility to claim them." We are not in accord about the status of women. Some find this problem reason to discourage their sons from considering a vocation in ordained ministry because their daughters cannot also serve. Many of today's priests (at least those over 50) were first encouraged toward ministry either by vowed religious women or their own mothers or sisters. In my years as a pastor, more than one mother told me that she would not encourage her sons to do what her daughters could not. This attitude is perhaps as troubling as the attitude of the bishops who apparently think that the short-term solution to fewer priests is more Sundays without Mass. Chicago's Cardinal Francis George's vision of the church, as explained in a *Commonweal* profile by Peter Feuerherd, is instructive and cautionary here: "When some people disagree with the 'church,' it is the church which should change, not the individual. But the church is given to change us, to be the place where Christ will change us" (January 16, 2004). Who would want to join the bishops before the judgment throne, explaining this time that the church did not change at my appointed pace, so it seemed we should stop celebrating the Eucharist until the boys heeded my wisdom and timetable?

These moms, my friends who told me of their decisions regarding their sons, have sometimes in recent years wanted to complain to me about some young priest or other. I have reminded them that they gave up their right to complain when they steered away the best and brightest from service in ordained ministry. (Wasn't it Stephen Stills who taught us to sing "Love the one you're with"?)

Some are concerned about the quality of our eucharistic celebrations with an aging presbyterate which is not seeing new recruits in numbers sufficient to replace those lost to death, retirement, and resignation. New York's late Cardinal John O'Connor often said in the years before his death that "The vocations crisis is over." It always seemed to me that it was over for him since where he was going, the church triumphant would have no shortage of angelic voices to sing the divine praises. We, however, who remain below are faced with "Sunday Celebrations in the Absence of a Priest" ("we feebly struggle, they in glory shine").

The genius of the Roman Rite will save us. The new *The General Instruction of the Roman Missal* (GIRM) makes it clear that it is "of the greatest importance" that the celebration of the Eucharist be arranged that all who take part, "according to the proper state of each, may derive from it more abundantly those fruits for the sake of which Christ the Lord instituted it" (17). Citing Vatican II's SCL, the new GIRM suggests that "This will best be accomplished if…the entire celebration is planned in such a way that it leads to a conscious, active, and full participation of the faithful both in body and in mind, a participation burning with faith, hope, and charity, of the sort which is desired by the church and demanded by the very nature of the celebration, and to which the Christian people have a right and duty by reason of their baptism" (18).

The brilliance of the guidelines ought to ensure that even the less gifted, surrounded by a gifted community of faith, can make the eucharistic event a true celebration of the emerging church. I went to a funeral recently in a lovely suburban church constructed with eight sides to recall the eighth day on which the Risen Christ makes all things new. There were greeters to welcome visitors to the parish, a fine sound system carefully attended by a worship director, an excellent couple of readers, a musician on piano and organ, a song leader up to the task of inviting and leading congregational song. All was nicely prepared and nicely celebrated. The aging pastor was neither an inspired preacher nor presider, but clearly a kind man who gathered the folks and appeared comfortable with the ministrations of all who prayed the funeral with him. Somehow this community kept their eyes on the prize and prayed very effectively with all of us who came as visitors for the day.

An issue today is that not all of us can keep our eyes on the prize. The bishop who preached the retreat for my classmates and me before our ordination to the priesthood came also to my home diocese to give a retreat for priests ten years later. At both, he told of his custom of arriving at parishes for visitation, and immediately checking the lavabo dish and towel and then usually departing for the local Kmart to buy what he considered a proper ewer and basin and a collection of terry cloth towels. I was amazed both times I heard his story that he would be so concerned about a very minor rite and its accouterments. I was then too timid, however, to ask how he addressed what the then current GIRM (1974) asked with regard to the eucharistic bread: "The nature of the sign demands that the material for the eucharistic celebration appear as actual food" (283). The current GIRM also notes that "The bread for celebrating the Eucharist must be made only from wheat, must be recently baked..." (320), and, "The meaning of the sign demands that the material for the eucharistic celebration truly have the appearance of food" (321). Perhaps that is a guideline that cannot be obeyed; how can true bread be made from wheat alone?

Unformed Critics

Another difficulty in many parishes is a flotilla of critics who are not always well versed in what ought to be, but clearly confident that their vision is compatible with what they presume the pope would want. Monica Hellwig, writing about College and University Theology or Religious Studies Departments and their critics, gives us a caution that applies to liturgical considerations and critics as well: "Sometimes, people who are not theologically trained take it upon themselves to condemn whatever sounds new or different. Such scrutiny should be left to those competent to judge." This issue of criticism is a serious problem for all who minister in the church. Many people who are not experts think that they are, and often when they suspect abuses, report first to the pope who they seem to presume is ready to pounce after having read their missives. These critics are, in my estimation, are also among the poor whom we will always have with us (cf. Matthew 26:11).

With or without the critics, the Instructions are clear that "All in the assembly gathered for Mass have an individual right and duty to contribute their participation in ways differing according to the diversity of their order and liturgical function." In order for each to participate, "all whether ministers or laypersons, should do all and only those parts that belong to them, so that the very arrangement of the celebration itself makes the church stand out as being formed in a structure of different orders and ministries" (58). It is important to read this instruction as it was intended: not so much that people should avoid usurping the priest's role but, rather, vice versa. The active role of the laity is not to be overshadowed, forgotten, relegated to insignificance, or confused with spectatorship. Remember the dignity that the first eucharistic prayer, the Roman Canon, gives to all in the worshiping assembly: "we, your people and your ministers." The ministers referred to therein are not only the ordained and vested concelebrants, but all God's people, claimed in baptism, and now gathered for praise and sustenance around the table which the Lord in tender mercy sets before us. Our developing spirituality as pastoral ministers insists, I think, that we work and pray to keep this truth in focus and in evidence.

The instruction notes that "In the celebration of Mass the faithful are a holy people, a people God has made his own, a royal priesthood: they give thanks to the Father and offer the victim not only through the hands of the priest but also together with him and learn to offer themselves." This one people "should become one body, whether by hearing the word of God, or joining in prayers and song, or above all by offering the sacrifice together and sharing together in the Lord's table" (62). The new *The General Instruction of the Roman Missal* summons us all, as each celebration of the Eucharist summons us, to a deeper realization of our communal call to holiness, reminding us of the dignity that is ours individually as baptized members of the body of Christ, and corporately as the body of Christ gathered Sunday by Sunday around book and table. When St. Augustine called the folks to communion, showing them the consecrated bread and wine, he said, "Behold what you are, become what you receive." That call to communion highlights both task and goal, dignity and duty. Apparently, then, we will always be practicing Catholics, holding the course, reading the Scriptures, immersing ourselves in prayer and sacrament, awaiting and anticipating the perfection that will be ours when, at last, we stand with all the heavenly choirs around the throne of grace. This vision of our own imperfection and of the glory that awaits us should quicken us in our ministry and encourage us in hope. Pondering these truths is not just the beginning of wisdom, but provides the building blocks for a strong and growing spirituality in and for ministry.

Next we will consider some challenges on the horizon for lay ministry and how we can better learn to share in the divinity of Christ.

For Reflection and Discussion

- Do you experience a "communal call to holiness" in your ministry? Why or why not?
- In what ways might you better "become what you receive"? How can you help others do this?

Challenges on the Horizon

*He was made man
that we might be made God.*   ❧ St. Athanasius

*...[M]ay we come to share
  in the divinity of Christ
who humbled himself to share in our humanity*
          ❧ Preparation of the gifts

We buried one of my high school teachers not so long ago, and at the wake I chatted briefly with a woman who had been a friend of his. She asked what I was doing these days, and told that I teach theology she asked sharply, "Do you teach that God is a man?" "No," I said, "I teach Catholic theology." I saw an equally unhappy friend of hers more recently when, some months ago, I presided at a reunion Mass for a Catholic institution. This friend, long absent from the eucharistic table, sat glumly through the service. Both of these women, intelligent and articulate, suffer from love-hate relationships with the church of their youth which they have largely abandoned in their disappointment. Dealing with folks in such pain is part of pastoral ministry for all of us. We can see them as challenges, frustrations, and disappointments, or we can choose to allow our interactions with them to become moments of special grace prompting us, as the second eucharistic prayer has us pray, to grow together in love. The latter approach will make us both vulnerable and strong.

There is, frankly, much to disappoint the critics of our decidedly imperfect communion. One hesitates to invoke Bill Clinton's "I feel your pain," but how to respond to those who so suffer is a problem. We live in a church scarred and stained by sin. Our leaders have disappointed us and, many charge, have squandered the church's authority in dealing with the issues surrounding the sexual abuse crisis. While wanting in justice to compensate victims, local churches then suffer the loss of programs and employees, services and real estate as millions of dollars are paid in reparation to scores of victims. One wonders who is driving the bus, the bishops or their lawyers. If resolution is beyond their immediate episcopal control, some critics charge that the bishops then turn their authority to what can be controlled: the norms for the celebration of the liturgy. Questions like "Who can fill the eucharistic cups?" or "At which moment may extraordinary ministers enter the sanctuary?" become issues of division and control more than helpful norms for a reverent celebration of Christ among us. Others, including the two women mentioned at the beginning of the chapter, charge that the church is beyond sexist in dealing with women.

If the church is as imperfect as it seems, why not move on? Is there a schism about to happen? Or are all these things simply evidence that we live under the curse of interesting times in a developing church?

The Faith Fix

These are truly times that try our souls, but one thing becomes increasingly clear as the church continues to grow: Peter's insight will provoke and sustain us through all the ages. He heroically articulated his faith even as any number of other disciples abandoned Jesus, to the Lord's disappointment. Jesus fed the enormous crowd with bread from heaven. They were delighted by the free food. But when he addressed them with the bread of life discourse, many of the disciples said, "This is a hard saying; who can listen to it?" Their attraction to

Jesus was based, it seems, on free food. When he suggested that the issue was bread for life and a new way of life, they were discouraged and went away. So, "Jesus said to the Twelve, 'Do you also wish to go away?'" Simon Peter answered him with heart-aching, graced-based loyalty, saying, "'Lord, to whom shall we go? You alone have the words of eternal life'" (John 6:60–69). Here is the mantra for troubled or interesting times, the inspiration of faith to quicken us in hope: "You alone have the words of eternal life."

And what do we ask for our leaders? Consider the opening prayer for the Mass for a council or synod: "Lord, / protector and ruler of your church, / fill your servants with a spirit of understanding, truth, and peace. / Help them to strive with all their hearts / to learn what is pleasing to you, and to follow it with all their strength."

About eleven years after the Lord's Ascension, squabbles in the church were so threatening "with no small dissension and debate" that "Paul and Barnabas and some of the others were appointed to go up to Jerusalem to the apostles and the elders" (Acts 15:2). At question was the relationship of the incipient church to the synagogue. Did new converts to the faith first have to become Jews? Must one keep kosher and must males submit to circumcision in order to follow Jesus? "The apostles and the elders were gathered together to consider this matter" (Acts 15:6). In announcing the decision, their letter reported that "it has seemed good to the Holy Spirit and to us" (Acts 15:28). And thus the nascent church begins to separate from the synagogue, a move more decisive and dramatic and with farther-reaching consequence than any act a council could promulgate today. Those dismayed by division, disagreement, and unpleasantness in the church in our own day should remember this lesson from Acts. The German Baptist minister Walter Rauschenbush, prophet of the American Social Gospel movement early in the last century, observed that the disciples could not keep pace with the sweep of the Master, fluttering where he soared. This is a truth which is observable in every age.

Historians tell us that fifty years of tumult follow every ecumenical council, but warn that the tumult will be extended in the wake of Vatican II because global communications make the conversation and the squabbles more accessible to greater numbers of participants. Sometimes, it seems, those who appear to oppose any movement or modification or *aggiornamento* (modernization) are the poor you will always have with you (see Matthew 26:11 and Mark 14:7). When we are at odds, when we have visions that seem incompatible, we might be called to realize that God's reign in all its fullness is still in our future.

Still Work to be Done

I suggested to the Duluth Benedictines before they recently elected their new prioress that there have been at least three times when Benedictines might have considered that they had accomplished the mission for which St. Benedict had initially called them together. St. Benedict, the father of western monasticism, seems to have realized that when what some historians call the Dark Ages was about to descend on Europe, learning would not be preserved in all of culture, but would be honored, preserved, and furthered in small enclaves, his monastic communities. Later, as the Renaissance flowered, Benedictines might have thought their work was done. But they remained faithful to their call, continued to seek truth, and enjoyed rejuvenation and redirection at Solemnes and elsewhere. Later yet they came to the New World and built the church here (Duluth's first bishop, James McGolrick, accurately and honestly said in tribute to Mother Scholastica Kerst, "She built my diocese"). The church securely established, once more they could have prayed, with Simeon, "Now, Lord, you may dismiss your servant in peace" (Luke 2:29).

Because there is a new day dawning with new challenges, I suggested to the Duluth sisters that they stand in the extraordinary gathering space of their Chapel of Our Lady Queen of Peace, put both their hands in the baptismal pool, and consider the mighty female saints who surround them in exquisite stained glass. Looking toward the altar, they see the book of the gospels enshrined on their left and the Holy Rule on their right. Lifting their eyes beyond the wall in front of them, they might be aware of the field of dreams behind in what they call the Valley of Silence where they have buried giants in the earth, the women who invited them into monastic communion. These were strong and demanding women who, even in all they suffered, were well aware that fragmentary realizations of the reign of God alone make life worth living.

Lowering their eyes, these sisters see the altar, Christ in our midst, borne up by the four angels they have placed at the corners. This table points to and connects with the table set for us in the reign of God before the foundation of the earth. Could one see these sights and, hands wet with baptismal water, proclaim that the work is done and that the time is at hand to fold up the tent and disappear into the night? "For the gifts and the call of God are irrevocable" (Romans 11:29).

Building the Church

Religious congregations are largely responsible for building the second-largest system (behind only the governmental systems) of educational enterprises, preschools through universities, as well as the second-largest health care network in the United States. And they did it working almost as volunteers, good stewards using their tiny stipends, spending and investing wisely to build for the reign of God. And they did it all without being accorded social and ecclesial status befitting such accomplishment.

When it is said that the sisters built the church in the New World, this is not just a metaphor, but also a literal truth. When I was privileged to be on the faculty of Caldwell College in New Jersey, I would invite students to stand at the classroom window, observing and admiring the Dominican sisters' motherhouse made of red brick with a wide porch and mahogany deck. These bricks had come by train up Bloomfield Avenue and were offloaded at the foot of the hill across the street from the birthplace of Grover Cleveland. The sisters, in full habit, carried the bricks by hand to their campus at the top of the hill to build their chapel, convent, and high school, with a college and health care facility to follow.

Such are the women who built the church in the New World. Thanks be to God.

Another Giant

Consider the story of Mother Alfred Moes, the foundress of the Joliet (Illinois) Franciscans in the late 1800s, a group dedicated to education and health care. At some point before Joliet was a diocese and when their territory was still part of the archdiocese of Chicago, the archbishop, annoyed for some reason with Mother Alfred, came to the motherhouse which shared a campus with what has become their University of St. Francis. The archbishop overstepped his authority and demanded that the sisters not re-elect Mother Alfred—and they acceded to his unreasonable request. Here is a woman who could have exploded with righteous anger. Instead, she apparently intuited what St. Augustine is alleged to have said, that anger has two lovely daughters, Hope and Courage. Mother Alfred left Joliet with those two virtuous daughters, and together with a small band of Sisters, started north.

When she got to Rochester, Minnesota, she met there some young doctors, brothers, who told her that the place needed a good hospital or clinic and while they were capable doctors, they did not quite know how to set up such an enterprise. "Okay, boys," she said, "you be the doctors and I'll take care of the rest." And thus was born the world-famous Mayo Clinic in the estimable shadow of the Rochester Franciscans on Assisi Heights. This story was first told to me by a recently deceased Joliet Franciscan; whenever I have heard the tale, the archbishop has no name (reminiscent of the rich man in the Lazarus story in Luke 16). Mother Alfred, however, will live in glory, "carried by the angels to Abraham's bosom" (Luke 16:22).

The sisters remember that her inspiration was Psalm 37: "Commit your ways to Yahweh, / Trust God, who will act. / Make your virtue clear as the light, / Your integrity as bright as noon." Sister Maria Pesavento, a later president of the Joliet Franciscans, writes that

"Mother Alfred's pioneering zeal does inspire us and we continue to listen to the Spirit and trust that God will act through each of us."

What are the challenges on the horizon for lay ministry? How can we think that they could be less painful or less glorious than those endured and enjoyed by our ancestors in the faith? God will give us grace to endure, to seek transformation in grace. And grace will lead us on: Flares of special grace will light our way. And there are among us even now new giants in the earth, filled with God's good Spirit, who will lead us to freedom.

Paul reminds us that "where the Spirit of the Lord is, there is freedom. And we all, with unveiled faces, beholding the glory of the Lord, are being changed into his likeness from one degree of glory to another; for this comes from the Lord who is the Spirit" (2 Corinthians 3:17–18).

And, "having this ministry by the mercy of God, we do not lose heart" (4:1), "For the gifts and the call of God are irrevocable" (Romans 11:29).

In concluding, we'll consider God's offer of covenant and our part in promoting and keeping that covenant as the foundation and the promise of our spiritual path.

For Reflection and Discussion

- What do you consider "the challenges on the horizon for lay ministry"?
- In what ways is your ministry a sign of *aggiornamento*? What does this mean in your own words?

CONCLUSION

Watch, Serve, Study, and Pray

I know that many of the faithful are voluntarily serving the Christian community in catechesis, in youth chaplaincies, in service to the sick. A large number carry out a mission entrusted to them by the bishop for a specific period, working in harmony with priests and deacons. The church rejoices in this, for she needs everyone's help in order to carry out her mission. As bishops, may you succeed in attracting and training true leaders. Show them your support, especially by offering them appropriate formation and spiritual guidance. May these persons feel that they are sent and backed by the diocesan church, with respect for difference and for the necessary complementarity of roles with the Christian flock whose shepherd is the bishop.
⁂ JOHN PAUL II, ADDRESS TO DUTCH BISHOPS ON THEIR AD LIMINA VISIT, 12 MARCH 2004

Give me discernment, that I may observe your law and keep it with all my heart. ⁂ PSALM 119:34

Today's pastoral ministers are much like Ezekiel the prophet as he stood in the center of the plain. We walk in a field filled with dry bones; we see them spread out in every direction. And we get to choose. We can say, "Our bones are dried up, our hope is lost, and we are cut off" (Ezekiel 37:11). Or, we can "say to the spirit, 'Thus says the Lord God: / From the four winds come, O spirit, / and breathe into [these bones] that they may come to life'" (37:5).

Atlanta's Archbishop Wilton J. Gregory reminds us that "If we look only at yesterday and at the models and triumphs that we enjoyed, we may not be able to see the great possibilities that tomorrow holds for us" (addressing the National Catholic Educational Association, April 18, 2006). Many of us tend to forget that we Christians live in a curious tension. We have one eye fixed on the past and one eye fixed on God's future; we live in the tension between those two times, praying always that God's kingdom which has begun will come in God's own good time to it fullness.

As we wait "in joyful hope for the coming of our Savior, Jesus Christ," we live in a certain ambiguity because life today is not as simple as it seemed in 1957. And it will not be that simple again. Paul VI of happy memory recognized that truth in 1968 when, in *Humanae vitae*, he wrote that "the recent course of human society and the concomitant changes have provoked new questions. The church cannot ignore these questions, for they concern matters intimately connected with the life and happiness of human beings" (1). Pope Paul considered that "this new state of things gives rise to new questions" (3). When he reports that he then "intently studied…as well as prayed constantly to God" (6), he becomes a model for us: watch, serve, study, and pray. In *The Courage to Be Catholic*, George Weigel writes that Pope Paul looked to the future for "a calmer cultural and ecclesiastical atmosphere" when "the truth…could be appreciated." We too await that time.

Like Paul VI, Cardinal Avery Dulles also notes a certain sense of ambiguity. He sees a lack of clarity flowing from the Second Vatican Council. He suggests that "Like most other councils, Vatican II issued a number of compromise statements. It intentionally spoke ambiguously on certain points, leaving to the future the achievement of greater clarity" ("The Basic Teaching of Vatican II," in *Sacred Adventure: Beginning Theological Study*, by William C. Graham). We must attend in these challenging days to the voices of Pope Paul and Cardinal Dulles. We will not serve the church well if we suggest that there is black and white where they may truly be shades of gray.

We who love the church will serve the church. We will recognize, as Cardinal Dulles points out, "In recent centuries it has been common to look upon the church as a divine institution without spot or wrinkle. Although Catholics have sometimes admitted the faults of individual believers, they have regarded the church itself as pure and holy. Vatican II, however, depicted the church in terms of the biblical image of the people of God. As we learn from Scripture, this people, though always sealed by its covenant relationship with God, was sometimes unfaithful. The *Constitution on the Church*, therefore, was able to admit, 'The church holding sinners in its embrace, is at the same time holy and always in need of being purified and incessantly pursues the path of penance and renewal' (LG 8). Furthermore, in the *Decree on Ecumenism*, the council declared, 'Christ summons the church, as it goes its pilgrim way, to that continual reformation of which it always has need, insofar as it is a human institution here on earth' (UR 6)."

This work of continual reformation is the call and task of the body of Christ, a work to which we together must commit ourselves and our church. We must always be on the lookout for models and examples to assist us. We see an example, a very effective piece of pastoral work and collaborative ministry, in the Second Book of Kings. The high priest Hilkiah informs the scribe, "I have found the book of the law in the temple of the Lord" (22:8). The scribe then informs the king to whom the law is read aloud. When the king hears the contents of the book of the law, he tears his garments, reforms his life, summons the elders and all the inhabitants of Jerusalem. He has the entire contents of the book of the covenant read out to them, thus reviving the terms of the covenant. And all the people stand as participants in the covenant. When we consider that story, we tend to pray with the psalmist: "Give me discernment, that I may observe your law and keep it with all my heart" (Psalm 119:34).

Beware of False Prophets

*Through Christ we have full confidence in God,
who has made us suitable ministers of his new covenant.*
                                 ❧ 2 CORINTHIANS 3:4,6

As we in pastoral ministry consider God's offer of covenant and our part in promoting and keeping it, we do well to remember the warning from Jesus in Matthew's gospel: "Beware of false prophets" (7:15). We tend to think, it seems to me, that false prophets are confined to an earlier age, perhaps all done in by Nicaea or Chalcedon or some other council from the distant past. Our temptation is to think that we are living the covenant quite nicely, thank you very much. But perhaps false prophets are with us in every age; they may well be the poor whom we will always have with us. Our American sense of individualism sometimes leads us, I think, to a false sense of our own importance.

Some college students now arrive on campus armed with the phrase "tyranny of relativism." This seems to mean that who or whatever does not agree with them, or with their understanding of what they think they may know or might have been taught of what the church teaches, is simply wrong, relatively speaking, and often heretical, and those who hold those wrong ideas have no rights. We faculty are often even more correct, or think we are, somehow seeming to believe that we know as much about everything as we knew about our own dissertations on the day of their defense.

The church's ministers are no exception in this regard. Too often, we think our own take on matters is the only take. Whether we are discussing liturgical translations, the timing of first penance or confirmation, catechetical or bedside approaches, the relationship of ordained to non-ordained, the role of women, inclusive language, or any number of other very real issues, we too often deny the church not only infallibility, but even the roles of *mater et magistra*, mother and teacher. When we assume this unfortunate stance of confusing our own perspective with the truth, we take on ourselves the mantle of infallibility in suggesting that the poor huddled masses should profit from our own superior, better understood, and more carefully nuanced view. This is not the humble stance of one who lives under the gospel.

St. Benedict, in his *Rule for Monasteries*, is attentive to the gospel in a manner we seek to emulate: "You have tested us, O God; / You have tried us as silver is tried by fire; / You have brought us into a snare; / You have laid afflictions on our back." St. Benedict then gives "72 Instruments of Good Works" which will rout out the temptation to false prophecy, arrogance, and judgmentalism from our own hearts. Number 62 is "To fulfill God's commandments daily in one's deeds." Number 67 is "To beware of haughtiness." Finally, Number 72: "Never to despair of God's mercy" (*Rule for Monasteries*, Chapter 4).

Conformed to Christ

We know that we cannot of ourselves take
 credit for anything,
for all of our sufficiency comes from God.
                                             ≫ 2 Corinthians 3:5

Formed in our lives and in our ministry by Scripture and the church's life of prayer, we will continue to pray: "Give me discernment, that I may observe your law and keep it with all my heart" (Psalm 119:34). This kind of discernment leads to fullness of life. Irenaeus, remember, tells us that the glory of God is (wo)man fully alive. In the treatise *Against Heresies*, Irenaeus writes, "The glory of God gives life." He also writes that Jesus reveals "to the human race visions of prophecy, the diversity of spiritual gifts, his own ways of ministry, the glorification of the Father, all in due order and harmony, at the appointed time and for our instruction." Not only that, but "where there is order, there us harmony, there is also correct timing; where there is correct timing, there is also advantage." It is for our benefit that God "has made such wonderful arrangements."

Understanding these things intellectually is one thing. To understand them and then to seek to craft our lives and ministry in response is to build a spirituality for pastoral ministry. This is the work of a lifetime. The sooner we begin, the closer we are to the reign of God.

Showing God's Glory

> *I am made glorious in the sight of the Lord,*
> *and my God is now my strength!*
> *It is too little, he says, for you to be my servant,*
> *to raise up the tribes of Jacob,*
> *and restore the survivors of Israel;*
> *I will make you a light to the nations,*
> *that my salvation may reach to the ends of the earth.*
> ❧ Isaiah 49:5–6

I pondered that truth about crafting our lives after I hired a bright, young, recent college graduate to give me a hand with some summer tasks before he went off to graduate school in the fall. On the first day of summer, we devoted ourselves to painting and (late) spring cleaning. At noon, I took him to our local diner out at Four Corners in Canosia Township. We entered, seated ourselves and were greeted in a heartbeat by an attractive young waitress who introduced herself by name. While she spoke to both of us, she looked only at my young companion. Zach is a handsome, sturdy and athletic young man with an engaging smile. She, lovely and vibrant, is perhaps seventeen or eighteen years old. The object of her gaze is an older man, twenty-two.

Had I not been so taken by her attention to the object of her stares, I would have felt a bit insulted at having been rendered invisible. She returned so often to our table, floating over to stand close to him, that I finally asked my young friend if he was aware of the chemical reaction that his very presence had occasioned. He nodded and smiled.

She returned. He flirted; she giggled. I remained invisible. She thought he should have dessert. He asked what she would recommend. She recited the list of her favorites and said he could safely choose any of them. I visited the men's room; she came back to see him twice in the minutes I was away. Paying the check, I tipped her generously for what I knew would soon work itself into either a homily or a reflective article.

Our first attraction to people is by their looks. Zack knew that. So did the waitress. But looks can deceive. Character cannot. Both of them can expect to have long lives ahead, but could squander or abuse their gifts and other people, later seeing themselves as the Prophet Isaiah first saw himself: "I thought I had toiled in vain, / and for nothing, uselessly, spent my strength" (49:4). Our waitress revealed herself as interested, innocent, and vulnerable. Zach revealed himself as kind and gracious. Many people move from this kind of beginning to disaster. I hope she will not, though I do not remember her name or know anything about her. I trust that Zach will not move to disaster. May God call them both to become like Isaiah whom God called by name from his mother's womb. Isaiah reports that God "made of me a sharp-edged sword / and concealed me in the shadow of his arm. / He made me a polished arrow, / in his quiver he hid me. / You are my servant, he said to me, / Israel, through whom I show my glory" (49:2–3).

Watching the dance between the young man and the young woman, and feeling hope for their futures, led me to reflect on the glorious vocation we share: showing in our lives the glory of God. Calling Isaiah to this vocation, God speaks: "It is too little, he says, for you to be my servant, / to raise up the tribes of Jacob, / and restore the survivors of Israel; / I will make you a light to the nations, / that my salvation may reach to the ends of the earth" (Isaiah 49:6).

The church employs Isaiah's words to speak of John the Baptizer, a giant in our tradition. John, the forerunner of Jesus, announced the light which brings salvation to all the world. Remember Luke's account of the visitation: "When Elizabeth heard Mary's greeting, the infant leaped in her womb" (Luke 1:41). Elizabeth, pregnant with John the Baptist, later tells Mary, pregnant with Jesus, "At the moment the sound of your greeting reached my ears, the infant in my womb leaped for joy" (Luke 1:44). John was about his task of announcing the coming of the Messiah even before his birth. Perhaps we can and should see the kind young man and lovely young woman, and ourselves too, in John's same tradition. We must then convince ourselves that joy, holiness, and wholesomeness are in fact far more common than we might first think. John Paul II clearly thought this in promoting so many as saints. If they can be holy, we can be holy. We too can announce the light which brings salvation to all the world, showing in our own lives the glory of God.

Is this not the best gift of the developing church to all of society: the sending forth of women and men who have learned in the school of the Lord's service, shaped into the polished arrow hidden in God's quiver of which Isaiah sang?

We in pastoral ministry, and in all parishes and institutions, are in the business of salvation, and all our efforts are directed to the pursuit of truth, and to moving and touching hearts. St. John Baptist de la Salle, founder of the Christian Brothers, writes that "God wills not only that all come to the knowledge of truth, but also that all be saved." According to de la Salle, procuring salvation meant seeking the total well-being of each student, and this process would begin with the teacher seeking to touch the hearts of the students entrusted to him or her. He speaks to each of us when he writes, "You carry out a work that requires you to touch hearts, but this you cannot do except by the Spirit of God."

Fr. Timothy Radcliffe, the former master general of the Dominican Order, writes in *Liturgy in a Postmodern World*, that the preacher today must do what Jesus did at the Last Supper. Everyone in pastoral ministry, I think, shares this same task defined by Radcliffe: "1) Jesus reaches out to his disciples in their individual puzzlement and confusion; 2) He gathers them into community; 3) He reaches beyond this community to the fullness of the kingdom." This is an apostolic task. We trust that God will continue to call those he chooses to undertake the task in every age; the apostolic power among us will make us ready to receive with joy the one whom we announce.

As we continue to develop a spirituality for ministry into which we might grow and by which we might continue to be formed, we can be confident that God will also raise up prophets in every age. If we cannot be the prophets for this new age and new movement, may we at least be touched, formed, called, consoled, and challenged by them.

Let those who are clothed in Christ say, "amen!"

For Reflection and Discussion

- In what ways does your own ministry give life to "dry bones"?
- What does saying "Amen" to Christ mean for you in practical terms?